Christian Scholarship…
for What?

Christian Scholarship…
for What?

CALVIN COLLEGE
GRAND RAPIDS, MICHIGAN

Calvin College, Grand Rapids, MI 49546

©2003 Calvin College
All rights reserved. Published in 2003
Printed in the United States of America

Library of Congress Catalog-in-Publication Control No. 2003104170

Felch, Susan M., ed.
       Christian Scholarship... for What?

ISBN 0-9727260-0-4

Table of Contents

Preface

On September 27-29, 2001 Calvin College concluded its 125th anniversary celebrations with an international, interdisciplinary conference centered on the topic, "Christian Scholarship... for What?" The title, a variation on Robert Lynd's provocative address to the American social science establishment in 1938, acknowledged that faith-based scholarship has come of age. It is no longer a question of whether we will produce, publish, and read Christian scholarship. Rather, we must turn our attention to improving such scholarship and thinking deeply about the purposes to which it is directed.

The conference, with its seven plenary and forty-seven concurrent sessions, attracted nearly 500 participants from around the world. Faculty, graduate students, church leaders, and interested laypersons from many different academic disciplines and Christian traditions gathered to think together about the project of Christian scholarship. This book includes the six major addresses, which were given at the conference. Many papers from the concurrent sessions may be found on the conference website: *http://www.calvin.edu /fss/125conf/sessions.htm*.

The conference itself was organized by the Seminars in Christian Scholarship program at Calvin College, ably assisted by a steering committee of Calvin faculty: Claudia Beversluis, James Bratt, Joel Carpenter, Janel Curry, David Van Baak, and John Witvliet. C. Stephen Evans gave valuable advice early in the planning process. Special thanks goes to the Seminars office staff: Anna Mae Bush, Krista Betts Van Dyk, Hope Bradley, and the incomparable Kerry Schutt Nason, who skillfully managed endless details. The conference was sponsored by grants from Calvin College, the Calvin Center for Christian Scholarship, *Books & Culture*, the William B. Eerdmans Publishing Company, and the Overseas Ministries Study Center.

This volume is indebted to the editorial efforts of Henry Baron and Krista Betts Van Dyk. It is dedicated to all those scholars – past, present, and future – who faithfully pursue their calling to research, read, and write to the glory of God.

Susan M. Felch
Director, Seminars in Christian Scholarship

Introduction

Joel Carpenter

This book, and the conference that produced it, have roots in two themes that have emerged in recent conversations about American academic and intellectual life. One of them focuses on how the nation's universities became bastions of secularity, and the other asks whether religious perspectives might play a significant role again in American academic life.

These two streams of inquiry converged not long ago in a provocative look at American higher education by historian George Marsden, *The Soul of the American University: From Protestant Establishment to Established Nonbelief* (Oxford, 1994). Marsden concluded this study with two proposals. The first was framed in response to the ongoing attack on scientific objectivity, an attack now described as postmodernism. If pluralism and tolerance were to be the chief values of academic life, Marsden asked, why not allow more academic freedom for the expression of traditional religious perspectives? His second proposal was a defense of the alternative academic commitments expressed by religiously founded colleges and universities, such as those maintained by Roman Catholics and conservative Protestants. Religious perspectives can enrich the life of the mind, Marsden argued, and the American secular academy would be the better for opening up its conversation to include them.

Initial responses to Marsden were sharply negative. Bruce Kuklick, a fellow historian of American thought, told a reporter from the *Chronicle of Higher Education* that Marsden's idea of Christian scholarship was "loony."[1] In a review of Marsden's book in *Lingua Franca,* sociologist Alan Wolfe argued against giving a welcome to religious ideas in scholarly discourse. Religion is too disruptive, he insisted, to add anything positive to the conversation. A year later, when Wolfe reviewed Marsden's next book, *The Outrageous Idea of Christian Scholarship* (Oxford, 1996), for the *Chronicle of Higher Education,* he

1

relented a bit. Perhaps religious thought could enrich the nation's learned discourse after all, he conceded.[2]

Apparently Wolfe continued to be fascinated with these questions, for in October of 2000, he published a cover story for the *Atlantic Monthly* on "The Opening of the Evangelical Mind." Wolfe still wondered how sincerely open such minds were, given their sponsoring colleges' religious requirements, but he conceded that at the best of these colleges, notably Wheaton and Calvin, "evangelical scholars are writing the books, publishing the journals, teaching the students, and sustaining the networks necessary to establish a presence in American academic life."[3] Indeed, the last 30 years have been a time of amazing growth in scholarship among evangelical Protestants. Evangelical scholars' efforts, moreover, have helped to prompt a rebirth of interest in the religious purposes of scholarship among Christians of other traditions.

The conference at Calvin College in late September of 2001 celebrated this robust and ecumenical scholarly movement, paused to consider the intrinsic value of Christian thinking, encouraged faith-based reflections on the responsibilities of Christian scholars within and beyond the academy, and sought to shape intellectual agendas for the future. The conference was planned to take advantage of two occasions for reflection: the beginning of a new century and the 125th anniversary of the founding of Calvin College and Calvin Theological Seminary.

There was another occasion that no one anticipated, however: the tragic events of September 11. Given the somber national mood of those days in September, the difficulty of moving about the country or indeed across the oceans, and the quite natural desire to stay at home with loved ones, the turnout for the conference was remarkable. For the 500 people who did come to the meeting, the mounting international crisis gave point and poignancy to the discussions about why Christians should engage in scholarship. More than once, speakers invoked the English Christian scholar, C.S. Lewis, whose 1939 chapel address, "Learning in War-Time," urged scholars to faithfully serve out their calling, which was strategically important to the much greater and longer-term struggle between good and evil.

The essays published in this volume first took shape as plenary addresses for the conference. They formed the backbone of the conversations that ranged across 47 concurrent sessions and more than 150 speakers, and in their range of tone, outlook and subject matter, they ably represent the whole conference.[4]

Richard Mouw, the president of Fuller Theological Seminary, gave the first plenary address, "Assessing Christian Scholarship: Where We've Been and Where We're Going." This was, as Mouw put it, the conference's "state of the union address." It featured both an encouraging account of the movement's progress and a call for "catholicity" – in fellowship among Christian scholars of many traditions, in range and purposes of inquiry, and in knowing and loving the fullness of the created reality. The call to Christian discipleship as a scholar demands these traits, Mouw insists, and also it demands hard work, cross-bearing sacrifices, and faithful persistence, especially in times like these, when learning must go on, even in war-time.

If anyone wondered whether the conference's catholicity would tend toward dullness, they were soon disabused of those thoughts. The next plenary speaker, Elizabeth Conde-Frazier of the Claremont School of Theology, speaking on "Christian Scholarship...for Whom?" argued that mainstream scholarship has been too narrow and self-referential in both its methods and its results. The post-Enlightenment ideal of rational abstraction is often at odds with Christian purposes, especially the faith's mission to the poor and oppressed. Conde-Frazier called for a relational and incarnational approach to scholarship that involves both the scholar and the people being studied. The aim of such research, she insisted, must be to redress injustice and to give witness to God's healing and blessing. Conde-Frazier, who has combined work as a professor and an inner-city pastor for many years, spoke of the frustration that people living in distressed neighborhoods feel when they are studied but not helped by scholars. The world needs Christian scholars, she urged, who are humble servants, who have the courage to be prophetic, and who will give of themselves for the poor and oppressed.

The next plenary speaker, essayist and novelist Marilynne Robinson, has described her work as "contrarian," and her speech, "Why Christian Scholarship Needs Story and Art," ran true to form. Her address focused on the oldest and perhaps the most obvious subject area for Christian scholarship, biblical studies. Robinson teaches the Bible as great literature, and she argued that to study it any other way is to do the Scriptures a grave injustice. The Bible's literary quality, she insisted, is the means by which it establishes truth and makes God's word live in one's heart and mind.

Robinson launched a relentless attack on the discipline of biblical criticism, claiming that its scholars were tone-deaf to the Bible's artistic integrity, larger theological themes, and literary power. Christian approaches to the study of the Bible ought to be looking at it whole, but modern biblical criticism is disintegrative. Critics' refusal to see the Bible as art, and their inability to attend to its aesthetic quality, constitute a new barbarism, she concluded. The sad irony is that many Protestants, whose Reformer ancestors insisted on the Bible's authority and perspicuity, now see it as a "veiled and doubtful text intelligible only to specialists." The most important task for Christian scholars today, she concluded, "is to acknowledge and redress the damage done by Christian scholarship" and rescue the study of the Bible from this new obscurantism.

The rhetorical waters of the next plenary session were much calmer, but the questions at hand ran deep. In his address on "Christian Scholarship and

Human Responsibility," John Hare, a philosophy professor at Calvin College, asked whether we can find an evolutionary basis for human morality. Hare claimed that humans have two gaps to reckon with in any attempt to develop coherent moral principles. The first is the gap between our desire for personal advantage and our sense of justice that runs beyond our own expediency. The second gap is between the demand to be moral and our actual performance. Contemporary moral philosophies, including ones deriving from evolutionary sociobiology and psychology, do not recognize the gap between our desires for advantage and for justice, and do not resolve the gap between our moral aspirations and our performance. Christian scholars have a major contribution to make, Hare concluded, by helping us understand the moral gaps we encounter and showing how they can be bridged without either lowering the demands morality makes or exaggerating our natural capacities to meet them.

Following on this discussion of the limits of evolutionary science for understanding human morality, the conference's attention turned next to what Christian scholarship has to do with the pursuit of science. Sir John Polkinghorne, a physicist and theologian from Cambridge University, argued that science is a self-contained endeavor with no need of assistance from other fields of inquiry, but Christianity gives deep and convincing answers to some fundamental questions that reflective scientists are driven to ask, such as "why is science possible?" Polkinghorne drew on his experience as a theoretical physicist to observe that the universe is "astonishingly rationally transparent... and rationally beautiful." Scientists also ask why the universe is so special; it had to be finely tuned from the start in order to produce life. That this process was happenstance, he observed, "defies belief."

Polkinghorne moved next from the questions behind science to the actual doing of science. He described how acts of personal judgment are basic to the practice of science. The enterprise deeply depends on the virtues of truthfulness and sharing of knowledge; the process of discovery relies on value-laden hunches (e.g. that definitive answers will come from elegant equations); and the application of scientific knowledge and technological power requires moral wisdom. Finally, Polkinghorne stressed that Christian thinking should be strongly supportive of science as a truth-seeking enterprise, one that does not provide the whole truth, but abundant truth nonetheless. Christians believe that truth is one, whether derived from the Book of Scripture or the Book of Nature. Christian scholars and Christian colleges, he concluded, should witness to the Church the importance of searching for the truth. They should witness to the Academy, moreover, the importance of acknowledging God as the source of all truth.

In the final plenary address, as in first one, the events of September 11 gave point and poignancy to the subject at hand, "Christian Scholarship and the Changing Center of World Christianity." Delivering this speech was Tite

Tiénou, the academic dean of Trinity Evangelical Divinity School. He was a last-minute substitute for the Ghanaian theologian, Kwame Bediako, whose North American itinerary was demolished in the wake of the terrorist attacks. Tiénou stressed that Christian scholarship must begin with an attitude of humility, for "the fear of God is the beginning of wisdom." Scholars best demonstrate humility, he argued, when they submit themselves to a community, in the midst of which they can increase their knowledge and mature their thought. Community, this West African theologian insisted, is not simply an African value, but fundamental to the Christian life, of living together as disciples, or learners.

If Christian scholarship is a shared task, Tiénou argued, then it is one in which Christians everywhere must share. He demonstrated, in dramatic fashion, the growing de-Christianization of the North Atlantic world and the rapid rise of Christianity elsewhere in the world, especially in Africa, Asia and Latin America. The importance of these facts for Christian scholars, Tiénou reasoned, is that while "the future of Christianity no longer depends on developments in the North," Christian thought coming from the South is still marginal. He critiqued Euro-American assumptions about what constitutes reliable knowledge and the North Atlantic world's centrality, the tendency to exploit the intellectual "raw material" of the South, and Northern intellectuals' inability to listen to others. Authentic Christian scholarship cannot be provincial, Tiénou concluded; it cannot afford to continue on the path of "arrogant regionalisms." To move forward together would require extra doses of humility, a discovery of the new scope of Christian community, and extra effort to link scholars across old boundaries in pursuit of common aims.

Before turning readers loose to explore these essays on their own, it may be helpful to suggest what they hold in common. Even in these widely disparate topics and approaches a set of shared traits emerge to help the reader understand the nature and aims of Christian scholarship.

First, Christian scholars endeavor to see the world whole. Beyond whatever focused work they do within their own fields of inquiry, they try to develop an understanding of the broader reality. Quoting the educational theologian Craig Dykstra, Richard Mouw urges Christian scholars to practice and teach the kind of seeing that can look "deeply into the reality of things and… love that reality."

Seeing the world whole means seeing God's handiwork, and humans' as well, in whole and integrative ways. As Marilyn Robinson pointedly insists, scholarship that splits, dissects and reduces, and then cannot see the whole for the parts, does not reveal God's truth, beauty and goodness. Neither does the study of humanity that does not participate in the struggle for justice and renewal, argues Elizabeth Conde-Frazier. Seeing the universe whole, Sir John Polkinghorne reminds us, reveals the rational beauty of the Creator's Mind.

And a whole-world approach to Christian scholarship will be shaped by the rich insights of the Global South, concludes Tite Tiénou.

Second, these scholars recognize that Christian scholarship is an act of humility and service. It begins with an attitude of humble reverence, Tiénou insists. It is a teacher's task, says Mouw. It calls us to put justice before self-interest, argues Hare, and to defend a morality that does the same. It serves the communities and people it studies, says Conde-Frazier. It humbly admits that its hold on the truth is not comprehensive or exhaustive, says Polkinghorne. And as Mouw reminds us, it respectfully acknowledges sources of wisdom outside its own particular heritage and incorporates them into its broader worldview.

To be a Christian scholar is to stand in awe of the Creator's handiwork, exclaims the scientist Polkinghorne. The world desperately needs scholars, says Mouw, who appreciate the "complex, created fullness" displayed in people worldwide, in all their diversity, and who grieve over the woundedness and brokenness of the world in its present state. For the Christian scholar, Robinson insists, the work itself must be "enacted faith, or love, or wonder." God calls us to "active, open, imaginative attentiveness – gracious attentiveness" to our fellow creatures and their works.

And finally, Christian scholarship, our authors insist, is a communal endeavor. We need each other in order to grow in knowledge as we share ideas, says Tiénou; our work will grow stronger and more mature as we submit it to the scrutiny of our brothers and sisters. Our work will have consequences, for good or ill, on the larger community of the faithful, as both Conde-Frazier and Robinson remind us. We need to consult them and respect the wisdom God gives them, Mouw insists.[5] And Christian scholars can powerfully serve the common good, insist both Hare and Polkinghorne, when they put forward their ethical values on the firmest possible grounds, those rooted in the love bestowed on us and the whole creation by the Heavenly Father.

There are a wealth of answers in these essays, and further questions as well, in response to the stated question of the conference. We offer these chapters, then, as conversation starters, in the hope that they will be of help to those engaged in the shared task of Christian scholarship.

---

[1] Kuklick is quoted in Carolyn J. Murphy, "Devout Professors on the Offensive," *The Chronicle of Higher Education,* 4 May 1994, A-18.

[2] Alan Wolfe, "Higher Learning," *Lingua Franca,* March/April 1996, 70-77; Wolfe, "A Welcome Revival of Religion in the Academy," *The Chronicle of Higher Education,* 19 September 1997, B4-5.

[3] Alan Wolfe, "The Opening of the Evangelical Mind," *The Atlantic Monthly,* October 2000, 58.

[4] Many of the papers presented in concurrent sessions are available on the conference's web page. Go to http://www.calvin.edu/fss/125conf/sessions.htm

[5] Especially in another work: Richard J. Mouw, *Consulting the Faithful: What Christian Intellectuals Can Learn from Popular Religion* (Grand Rapids: Eerdmans, 1994).

Assessing Christian Scholarship: Where We've Been and Where We're Going

Richard J. Mouw

In their book-length study of academic leadership, Michael D. Cohen and James G. March make a rather cynical comment about the kinds of Big Picture speeches that are regularly given by academic presidents. "Almost any educated person," they observe, "can deliver a lecture entitled 'The Goals of the University.' " But, they quickly add, there are very few people who will voluntarily sit through that kind of lecture. This is so, they judge, because, "[f]or the most part, such lectures and their companion essays are well-intentioned exercises in social rhetoric, with little operational content."[1]

I am glad they added the "for the most part" clause, because I am not convinced that Big Picture academic addresses are useless exercises. Indeed, given the events of recent weeks, Big Picture questions about how our work as scholars fits into the larger scheme of things seem especially poignant. I began working on this address long before the events of September 11, 2001, but since that dreadful day I have re-worked this speech in a state of mind and heart that is well described by the old invitation" hymn.

> Just as I am, though tossed about,
> with many a conflict, many a doubt,
> fightings and fears, within, without…[2]

While I will not spend most of my time here directly addressing practical issues relating to the present crisis, I hope it will be obvious that I do believe that our agenda as Christian scholars cannot help but be shaped by sensitivities to the "tossed about" condition of our immediate cultural context.

Actually, the Big Picture topic that I have been assigned has some obvious similarities to the content of a political "State of the Union" address. Typically the people who compose those speeches employ some partisan rhetoric, while also striving at crucial points to transcend partisan concerns in order to say something helpful about the good of the whole. I will follow that pattern here.

I will begin by speaking quite unashamedly as a member of the evangelical party's Kuyperian caucus, and having been encouraged by the conference planners to speak freely in the first person, in good evangelical fashion I will even take a little time to offer a brief version of my scholarly testimony. But I will also get around to offering some observations about the larger "state of the union" in Christian scholarship as such.

Emerging from Anti-intellectualism

First, then, my testimony.

During my undergraduate days, I went through a serious spiritual crisis in struggling with the life of the mind. My problem was that I was actually enjoying my liberal arts education – and especially my philosophy courses. I had even started thinking that maybe I wanted to spend the rest of my life studying and teaching that kind of thing.

This wasn't the way it was supposed to be. I was an evangelical preacher's son, and the pressure to follow in my father's footsteps was strong. In my spiritual environs, higher education was something that you suffered through in order to be able to get on with the Lord's real work: the urgent business of proclaiming the Gospel in all of its simplicity and power. The rhetoric of anti-intellectualism ran wild in the sermons that I heard at evangelistic meetings and summer Bible conferences. I remember clearly the loud "amens" that one traveling revival preacher evoked when he told us that, in contrast to what he had learned in the few seminary courses he had taken, "you don't need exegesis, you just need Jesus!" All that the worldly intellectuals have to offer, another pulpiteer warned us, is a bunch of "fool-osophies." And there was much more: "Education is a good thing only if you get the victory over it"; "The only school any Christian needs to attend is the Holy Ghost's school of the Bible." And so on.

But here I was, a sophomore in college, and I was actually finding my studies to be an exciting intellectual adventure. What was happening to me? I worried much that I was not only disappointing my family's hopes for me, but that I was also rebelling against the plans that the Lord himself had for my life.

Then one day a guest speaker came to the Christian college campus where I was studying. Frank Gaebelein, the son of the editor of the Scofield Bible, was a well-known evangelical leader in his own right. He wrote learned articles in Christian magazines and was the headmaster of The Stony Brook School, a prestigious Christian prep school.

His lecture, entitled "The Christian's Intellectual Life," gave me a new perspective on the struggles I had been having. Four decades later, I still remember some of his remarks (although I don't need to rely on memory alone, since the lecture was later published in a book of Gaebelein's essays). In contrast to the secularist outlook, said Gaebelein, Christians must insist that "our intellectual life is infused with faith." But that does not mean that Christian intellectual activity is an easy thing. We must pay a price if we are to use our minds to glorify God. "And the price will not come down. It is nothing less than the discipline of self-restraint and plain hard work."[3]

Today that strikes me as a simple and obvious message, but it had a deep impact on me at the time. I am grateful that I heard Gaebelein's talk at a point in my life when I desperately needed Christian encouragement that I did not have to make a choice between a life devoted to scholarship and obedience to the Lord. The call to cultivate a disciplined mind that struggled with deep intellectual challenges could itself be a divine summons.

I tell that story to illustrate the pervasive anti-intellectualism that characterized evangelical Christianity in the earlier decades of the twentieth century. But the story also points to changes that had begun to occur around mid-century. Frank Gaebelein was only one of many "neo-evangelical" leaders who were doing their part to promote a new appreciation of the scholarly enterprise – a movement that was given much visibility by the appearance of *Christianity Today* in 1956. As I looked for more concrete guidance for the Christian intellectual quest, I received most of my inspiration from those thinkers who insisted that all intellectual activity is guided by presuppositions that are not themselves "provable" by a straightforward appeal to rational criteria, and that Christian thought at its best will be self-consciously explicit about its intellectual starting-points. This way of conceiving the Christian scholarly project was developed most systematically by those who were influenced by the Kuyperian strand of Dutch Calvinism: in my case I was helped early on by reading Cornelius Van Til, Herman Dooyeweerd, and Henry Zylstra. But that basic picture of the scholarly life was also reinforced by the writings of Carl Henry, Edward John Carnell, Bernard Ramm, and others in the more Anglo-American strand of evangelicalism.

At the time, the notion that intellectual activity is inevitably guided by pre-rational commitments was not the sort of thing that was taken seriously in the mainstream academy. But the climate began to change during the 1960s with the emergence at the universities of the radical student movement. As a graduate student during that decade, I participated in various political protest movements, which in their most extreme form insisted that the scholarly agenda in the university world was pervasively guided by racial and class biases, as well as by the unacknowledged economic interests of "the military-industrial complex" – but which, even in their more modest expressions, displayed much skepticism about the long-standing presumption that the intellectual life was, when properly pursued, a "neutral" activity.

It would take a decade or so before the angry political attacks on "rational neutrality" would take the form of more calmly articulated arguments – of the sort that Alasdair MacIntyre laid out in his analysis of "the failure of the

Enlightenment project."[4] But when I joined the Calvin faculty in 1968, I think many of us already sensed some sort of connection between the current political critique and the themes that had long been argued by Christian presuppositionalists. Not that we thought that the Students for a Democratic Society, in their attacks on the "neutrality" of the university, were simply repeating what the Kuyperians had been saying all along. Hardly. But we were very much aware of a new mood in the academy, an emerging climate of opinion in which our kind of Christian perspective on the intellectual life, one that had thus far been developed on the margins of mainstream scholarship, could now be re-worked with the realistic expectation that our way of viewing things could gain a new hearing in the larger intellectual community.

And this new mood of self-confidence influenced the ways we viewed long-standing intra-Christian disagreements. I am convinced that many of our past debates about the details of a Christian perspective had an important subtext: namely, the question of who would exercise a kind of cognitive control over the maintenance of "church-world" boundaries within a given subculture.

Several years ago, Michael Hakkenberg published a fascinating study of a dispute that raged for a few years in Orthodox Presbyterian circles between two philosopher-theologians, Cornelius Van Til and Gordon Clark.[5] On the face of it, the argument looks like the kind of thing that would only be interesting to people who enjoy fairly technical theological debates. The controversy was referred to as the debate over "the doctrine of the incomprehensibility of God," with Clark arguing that there is an important univocal element that characterizes the relationship between human and divine knowledge, and Van Til insisting that the relationship is purely analogical. A fascinating debate to some of us, actually, but it is hard to comprehend the passion with which it was conducted, and the winner-take-all stakes: Clark found himself increasingly embattled and eventually left the denomination.

It seems obvious that more was at issue in those discussions than a specific point of technical theology. As Hakkenberg observes, the two sides were actually battling over the cultural direction of the denomination. By proposing a formulation that had some continuities with Arminian theology, Clark was encouraging a Calvinism that would be open to active cooperation with the broader evangelical community. Van Til's rather stark contrast between divine and human knowledge, on the other hand, would reinforce a similarly stark contrast between the denomination's thought patterns and those of the rest of the Christian world.

Much the same spirit characterized the heated arguments in Christian Reformed scholarly circles from the 1950s into the 1970s between the Dooyeweerdian Kuyperians and the Kuyperians of a looser, non-Dooyeweerdian variety: the struggle was between competing models for shaping the patterns of cooperation and/or separation of an ethnic community that was at the time thinking much about its relationship to the North American context.

Joining the Broader Community of Christian Scholarship

These battles for "internal" intellectual hegemony take place in communities that have been defining themselves for the most part *over against* the larger intellectual culture. They cease to have that particular social meaning when the group as a whole decides to shape more cooperative strategies within that larger context. This strikes me as what has happened to most evangelical scholars over the past few decades. We have decided to make our Christian voice known, not by way of a critique that is directed toward the mainstream academy from the intellectual margins, but by forming coalitions and networks within that mainstream academy. Having made that decision, the perspectives that we set forth in our intra-Christian arguments – while certainly still interesting enough to keep debating – are no longer weapons used in disputes over cultural direction. Rather, they provide the currency that facilitates our entrance into a larger, and much friendlier, conversation with people with whom we disagree on matters major and minor.

It is one of the great blessings of my life to have had the privilege of being a member of the Calvin College community in those early days of evangelical scholarly *aggiornamento*. But the blessing was not restricted to the "internal" life of this campus. The excitement had much to do with a strong sense of the need to reach out to other evangelicals, and indeed to colleagues in the broader Christian community, as we attempted to address in more direct ways the larger world of scholarship. There was a new enthusiasm for learning from like-minded folks at Wheaton and other evangelical colleges, as well as from scholars in the Protestant mainline and those on Roman Catholic campuses. In short, in some mysterious way, a new confidence about the relevance of our own unique Kuyperian tradition to the broader contemporary dialogue was accompanied by a new appreciation for the catholicity of the Christian scholarly enterprise.

The growing awareness of being a part of a broader Christian scholarly movement has helped many of us work on some other defects that have, in the past, inhibited a healthy intellectual outlook. Evangelicalism's long-standing problems with the intellectual life were not only due to a strong anti-intellectualism. We have had difficulties in cultivating healthy academic habits even when we have successfully overcome our suspicions of the intellect as such.

One key problem has been our tendency toward *triumphalism*. The intellectual version of this feature has a parallel in evangelical attitudes toward the public square. We pietist types have a long history of an other-worldly mentality that encourages a conscious retreat from any active involvement in public life. The problem is that when we do get around to convincing ourselves that this is an unhealthy posture, we tend to move in the direction of a political triumphalism. We either abandon the public square or we try to take it over. When we stop singing, "This world is not my home, I'm just a-passing through," we immediately start singing, "Shine Jesus, shine, fill this land with the Father's glory." The option of a modest participation in public life, cooperating as much as possible with other groups for admittedly partial gains toward the common good, usually does not seem to strike us as a viable option.

A similar pattern has characterized our intellectual efforts. Either we consign ourselves to the margins of the academy, or we entertain hopes of achieving major intellectual victories. These strong triumphalist themes can be found in the writings of some of the mid-twentieth century "neo-evangelical" scholars – a habit of mind that greatly disturbed Edward John Carnell, for example. In a letter that Carnell wrote in 1954 to Harold John Ockenga about the possibility of succeeding Ockenga as Fuller Seminary's president (which he did), Carnell offered this candid report of a recent discussion among his Fuller colleagues:

> Stress was made of the fact that the new president ought to lead the faculty out in the publication of world-shaking literature. Has it never occurred to them that in the seven years they have had to show deeds rather than words, that no one man on this faculty has published as much as one article in a scholarly journal; let alone publishing a book with a major house. This faculty has an amazing sense of its own virtues. If I were president, I would only irritate them; for I refuse to be party to their fantastic schemes.[6]

It is fair to say, I think, that we evangelicals have become less grandiose in our scholarly designs in recent decades. And, ironically, in the process of abandoning the kinds of "fantastic schemes" that irritated Carnell, we have actually begun to produce the kind of scholarship whose absence was so obvious to him. The dreams of evangelical scholarly triumphs – spelled out in the not so distant past, for example, in visions of a major North American evangelical university – have been replaced by commitments to small-scale scholarly cooperative projects. A crucial phenomenon here has been – to use a contemporary buzzword that nonetheless has considerable operational value – networking. Evangelicals have helped form discipline-related groups: Faith and History, Christianity and Literature, Christian Philosophy, Christian Psychology, and so on. Topics of common concern have been explored in subsections of the major academic conventions. Liberal arts colleges have co-sponsored faculty development seminars. There has been the important process that I like to think of as the Lilly-ing of the guilds, where support from major foundations, such as the Lilly Endowment and The Pew Charitable Trusts, has provided significant funding for faith-based scholarly projects. There has been a laudable proliferation in recent years of special centers and institutes devoted to religious research on a variety of Protestant and Catholic campuses. And new periodicals, such as *Books & Culture*, have provided opportunities for broad ranging Christian cultural commentary.

In all this, many of us have had to let go of stereotypes we have employed in describing the views of other traditions of Christian scholarship. When we are intent upon maintaining a strict sense of separation from other Christian communities, our favorite ways of depicting other perspectives function as boundary-preserving markers that reinforce the kind of cognitive hegemony that I mentioned earlier. The syndrome is not unlike what the Freudians call "the narcissism of minor differences" – where people who are not really all that far apart exaggerate their disagreements. From a spiritual perspective, this sort of thing is sinful, a violation of the commandment not to bear false witness against our neighbors. Whatever else we might say about the current state of Christian scholarship, it seems obvious to me that there is a lot less sinning of this sort going on these days.

Protestant-Roman Catholic Relationships

One area where the sin of bearing false witness against scholarly Christian neighbors has greatly diminished is in Protestant-Roman Catholic relationships. The gains here have been facilitated in part by significant changes that have been occurring in the Roman Catholic academy.

In a recent article on the current situation in Catholic higher education, Monika Hellwig offers a brief but helpful overview of trends during the past half-century or so. In the 1950s, she argues, Catholic campuses typically went about their business in a rather "inattentive" manner:

> It was so obvious what it meant to be Catholic in higher education that few bothered to think about it. Chapel, prayer before class, crucifixes on the walls, classes on Thomistic philosophy, religion lessons located somewhere between catechism and seminary, no meat on Friday and confessions heard on Saturday – the externals were all in place, so one did not need to question what constituted the inner reality. [7]

Things began to change in the 1960s with shifting governance patterns and curricular revisions, to say nothing of the new mood fostered by the Second Vatican Council. Both institutions and individual scholars, says Hellwig, "were enjoying a kind of spiritual adolescence – an awakening of personal discernment and a deeper level of personal responsibility." As Hellwig sees things, these were healthy developments, as many Catholic scholars were seeking "[c]reative expressions of faith in quest of understanding." The healthy process has not been helped, says Hellwig, by what she describes as – and she is alluding here to the ongoing debates stirred up by the Vatican document *Ex Corde Ecclesiae* – "increasingly shrill demands from the Roman Curia that universities around the world be reshaped to fit inside the predetermined rules."[8]

For all of the current tensions, though, Hellwig offers a basically positive assessment of the state of things in the Catholic intellectual world:

> Catholic higher education is alive and well in its corporate expression on our campuses – not everywhere, not always, not in every professor or administrator, but predominately and very actively. Where the religious congregations are diminishing, a new generation of lay leadership has come to the helm with considerable energy, good will and sense of purpose and direction.[9]

I think this is an important observation for all of us, Catholic or not, to reflect upon seriously as we attempt to understand the present "state of the union" in Christian scholarship. For one thing, Hellwig's nuanced comments apply nicely to all of our communities – Catholic, old-line Protestant, evangelical, Orthodox. *Christian scholarly activity is in fairly good shape:* to use Hellwig's exact words, "not everywhere, not always, not in every professor or administrator, but predominately and very actively." The nuances are certainly important for an assessment of the evangelical situation. In spite of my hopeful mood, I do take seriously the concerns expressed by two of my good friends in books they have written in the last ten years: Mark Noll is right to worry about continuing manifestations of anti-intellectualism in the evangelical movement;[10] and George Marsden's account of a continuing hostility toward Christian scholarship in the larger academy[11] is an important reality check. But for all of that, Christian scholarship is – to be sure, "not everywhere, not always" – in fairly good shape.

Monika Hellwig's passing reference to the role of the Catholic laity in all of this also has a more general application. Referring to the decline in vocations to Catholic religious orders during the past several decades, she observes that "a new generation of lay leadership has come to the helm with considerable energy, good will and sense of purpose and direction." As an outsider to the Catholic debates over *Ex Corde Ecclesiae*, I worry about two misguided impressions given, especially by the ecclesiastical hierarchy: one is that the health of Catholic higher education depends primarily on what *theologians* teach and write about; and the other is that since there are confused things being said by some prominent theologians, this means that there is a dangerous decline in the state of Roman Catholic thought.

The fact is that, for many of us, much of the energetic activity that has been taking place in recent Roman Catholic scholarship has been happening outside of Catholic seminaries and theology departments. The action has taken place primarily in philosophy, literature, history, and the social and natural sciences.

Let me generalize from that. Recent activity in Christian scholarship in general has been an impressive "ecumenical" phenomenon, one that has been for the most part conducted by laity representing the various traditions. People who write about the alleged decline of the ecumenical movement in the past few decades simply have not been paying attention to, say, the Society of Christian Philosophers, the Faith and History gatherings, and other configurations of Christian scholarly activity in a variety of disciplines and interdisciplinary explorations where there is not only high-level scholarly dialogue, but also worship and the sharing of personal pilgrimage stories. Indeed, this conference is a good case in point for that phenomenon. This gathering – with people from many different Christian communities – manifests a spirit of cooperation and common purpose that does not match up in any neat manner with the official pronouncements that are operative in Calvin College's sponsoring denomination regarding the traditions represented here.

The Contextualization Mandate

One of the important lessons we have been learning in recent years, of course, is that it is not sufficient to spell out the different perspectives within the Christian community solely with reference to the categories that have long been employed in mapping Christian diversity. This lesson was impressed upon me in a graphic way a few decades ago when I was invited to lead a workshop at a large conference on urban ministry. In order to insure some uniformity in the format of the workshops, the conference planners asked each leader to choose a title that fit the following formula: "A _____ theological perspective on urban _____." The first blank was meant to be filled in with a label that identified the leader's theological perspective; the second was for singling out the specific area of urban life that would be discussed. I had no difficulty filling in the blanks: I wrote "Reformed" for my theological perspective and "politics" for my area of focus.

When I received the official program for the conference, however, I was struck by the ways in which various workshop leaders identified their theological perspectives. Some had chosen, as I had, a label that had long had some currency in theological discussion: "A Lutheran theological perspective on urban law," "A Catholic theological perspective on urban education," "A Mennonite theological perspective on urban community." But others chose very different sorts of labels: "A black theological perspective on urban family life," "A feminist theological perspective on urban economics," "An Asian-American theological perspective on urban church life."

What took me by surprise then has become commonplace now in theological discussion: the labels associated with what we have come to think of as "identity theologies" – ethnic, gender, and national characteristics – are now widely acknowledged to have theological relevance. The significance of this newer labeling system was impressed upon me with even more poignancy not long afterward, when I attended an ecumenical consultation that focused on the question of eucharistic fellowship. When the time for discussion groups came, the delegates were divided into the standard confessional groups: Catholic, Orthodox, Anglican, Free Church, and so on. I was in the Reformed group, and at the outset of our small group discussion the one woman member described her discomfort at being in our group: "In my church," she said, "I am not allowed to officiate at the communion service. Because of that, I feel that I have much more in common with the Catholic nun in the next room than I do with you men." The one black member of our group quickly joined her protest: "In my part of the country, communion services are still racially segregated – and that's true whether your theology is Reformed or Catholic or Methodist!"

People who claim the newer "identity" labels often mean to be protesting against a "North Atlantic" or "northern hemisphere" understanding of theology, where the agenda is set in terms of the classical topics debated by and among the Orthodox, Catholic, and various Protestant traditions. This agenda is challenged by an insistence that race, gender, class, and geography have an important theological relevance. The term "contextualization," like its close kin "indigenization," is a theme that is emphasized by thinkers who want to draw our attention to the different ways in which the Christian message is received, appropriated, and interpreted in a variety of cultural contexts. It is not uncommon for such thinkers to ask that we take an honest and critical look at the ways in which the transmission of the Gospel to the non-Western world has been weighed down by a close association with colonialist programs, as well as with the values of a technocratic-scientific worldview.

Nor has this kind of emphasis been viewed as necessarily hostile to the core beliefs of traditional Christian communities. Indeed, contextualization issues have received much positive attention from thinkers who represent the more orthodox theological perspectives, especially evangelicals and Roman Catholics; it is the representatives of these traditions who have also been in the forefront of recent missionary activity, continuing to evangelize persons from non-Christian groups long after that has ceased to be a high-priority activity among mainline Protestants. Consequently, the more conservative Christian groups have been forced to struggle with contextualization issues because of the challenges presented to them by their own converts, who often combine a deep interest in cross-cultural questions with a strong commitment to theological orthodoxy.

To repeat: it is a good thing that Christian thinkers have become sensitive to such matters. My examples here have been primarily theological, but it should be obvious that the contextualization mandate goes out to all of us, no matter what our areas of scholarly specialization are. In this regard we owe much to the larger secular academy where, throughout the humanities and the social sciences in recent decades, important segments of the human race, long ignored in our studies of the human experience, have been given voice.

We have begun to learn new things about the lives of peasants as well as the policies of prime ministers, about families who lived in slave quarters as well as the affairs of artists and poets, about the daily struggles of women who lived in cloistered convents as well as the dictates of queens and empresses.

We Christians have our own important contributions to make as we join our efforts to those of other scholars who are seeking to cultivate these broader understandings. Our Christian scholarly discussions are rooted in a global community that is held together by a deep spiritual kinship. The relationship between these spiritual bonds and our common academic calling is especially important to explore these days, when so much of multiculturalism in the academy seems to pattern itself after the diversity of Babel, where racial and ethnic groups were plagued by a confusion of tongues that made it difficult for them to understand each other. But we know that there is a biblical alternative to the divisiveness and angry demands that characterize the multiculturalism of Babel. It is the multiculturalism of Pentecost where, by the power of the creating and redeeming Spirit of God, people of many nations were able to hear together a new message of unity:

> Amazed and astonished, they asked, "Are not all these who are speaking Galileans? And how is it that we hear, each of us, in our own native language? Parthians, Medes, Elamites, and residents of Mesopotamia, Judea and Cappadocia, Pontus and Asia, Phrygia and Pamphylia, Egypt and the parts of Libya belonging to Cyrene, and visitors from Rome, both Jews and proselytes, Cretans and Arabs – in our own languages we hear them speaking about God's deeds of power." (Acts 2:7-11 New Revised Standard Version)

And the question that they went on immediately to ask on that day of Pentecost is one that we Christian academics need to ask for our own context: "All were amazed and perplexed, saying to one another, 'What does this mean?'" (Acts 2:12 NRSV) This does mean some important things for the way we shape our individual and collective scholarly pursuits, as we prepare – even as Christian scholars – to join the celestial choir who will someday sing the great victory hymn of Revelation 5:

> You are worthy to take the scroll and to open its seals,
> for you were slaughtered and by your blood you ransomed for God
>   saints from every tribe and language and people and nation;
> you have made them to be a kingdom and priests serving our God,
>   and they will reign on the earth. (Revelation 5:9-10 NRSV)

To be sure, our cross-cultural dialogues, in which we take our social-location identities seriously, should not ignore the issues that have also been associated with the aforementioned "North Atlantic" labels. African Catholics will formulate their views on many issues differently than their colleagues in the African Independent churches, African American Holiness Christians differently than African American Baptists, Korean Presbyterians differently than Korean Methodists, Latino Lutherans differently than Latino Pentecostals, and so on. Both sets of labels are important. Our discussions together need to be more far-ranging and complex than we thought they needed to be in the past.

Honoring Distinctives and Embracing a Common Calling

I, for one, hope that these discussions will not ignore some continuing significant disagreements among us. I know, of course, that I have come to hold my own Kuyperian perspective a little more loosely than I would have thought possible in the past. On many important subjects I have had to learn what Jeffrey Stout refers to as the practice of *bricolage*: a kind of intellectual puttering, a piecing of things together by drawing on whatever odds and ends are available.[12] Nor am I ashamed of my *bricolage* habits. I am still a rather traditional Calvinist, but my Calvinism is not, nor should it be, of the exact vintage of my forebearers. I have had many more opportunities than they could have imagined to enter into serious dialogue with Anabaptists, Lutherans, Pentecostals, Roman Catholics, Eastern Orthodox, and Jews; and I have come away from those encounters with new theological odds and ends that I have simply been forced to incorporate into my understanding of reality. Much the same has happened to me as a grandson of Dutch immigrants who has spent a few decades living in predominantly African-American neighborhoods, and who now presides over a Pacific Rim seminary whose students come from sixty nations. The odds and ends accumulate, and the kind of *bricolage* that has transformed my life has been inevitable – and exciting.

But for all of that, I am still a convinced adherent to my specific tradition. I have no inclinations to embrace a "generic" Christian understanding of things. For evangelistic and apologetic and cooperative purposes, I am happy to endorse the basic non-negotiable tenets of "mere Christianity." But it is difficult for me to think too long about the "mere-ness" without placing myself within a very particularistic tradition of Christian thought and action. And, frankly, I long for dialogue partners who have found it necessary, in a similar manner, to combine a healthy propensity for *bricolage* with a firm commitment to the traditions that have nurtured them.

Some of us, for example, are firmly convinced that, to use Nicholas Wolterstorff's well-known formulation, the Christian weighing and forming of the theories that guide our scholarly efforts must be done with a clear acknowledgement of the role of explicitly Christian control beliefs.[13] Others of us question the need for this "Christian content" approach to assessing theoretical models and frameworks. The issues here are of extreme importance. We control-belief advocates need regularly to be warned by our Christian colleagues of the danger of too much suspicion about the assumptions made by secularist scholars. But the defenders of a broad expanse of "common ground" between Christian and non-Christian thought need to be reminded of the dangers of various intellectual reductionisms in a cultural climate where there is all too much "reducing" of human beings going on. The arguments about such matters need to be continued.

To be sure, nothing that I have said is meant to rule out serious conversations about the common elements of our work as Christian scholars from different traditions. Much of the task of Christian scholarship does not consist in engaging in perspectival debates with other Christians, or engaging in cross-cultural dialogue, or thinking about basic presuppositions, or participating in grand projects of interdisciplinary significance. Much of what we do flows from our ongoing attempts to master a field of inquiry, and from our efforts to impart what we have learned to the students in our classes, as well as to the colleagues whose interests lie most closely to our own. I accept that fact and have no intention here of launching into a critique of specialization or of the narrowness of much of our everyday scholarly focus. To return for a moment to the personal testimony I offered earlier, the message that was most encouraging to me at the beginning of my own scholarly quest was not a grandiose call to think large and profound thoughts, but rather the insistence that I attempt to bring glory to the Lord with my mind by, in Frank Gaebelein's words, "nothing less than the discipline of self-restraint and plain hard work." This is certainly a non-negotiable matter for all that deserves to be called Christian scholarship.

But there must be more. A while back, my son told me about a woman in the university town where he studies who distributed a business card listing the services that she offered to the community. Along with such specialties as herbal healing, therapeutic massage, and the like, she described herself as an "ontological coach." I don't know how she would have further spelled out that item in her job description, but it does strike me that Christian scholarship will inevitably include an ontological coaching function. In addition to our specific areas of expertise, we all need to maintain a second specialty in the study of being-in-general, in the nature of reality.

In one of the delightful talks that he gave to a group gathered in the studio of a sculptor friend, the philosopher Josef Pieper reported that the pre-Socratic Athenian thinker Anaxagoras, while engaging in a catechetical type exercise, answered the question, "Why are you here on earth?" with the stark reply, "To behold." Pieper applied Anaxagoras' comment to the artistic task, but it holds as well for the work of the Christian scholar. We must engage in beholding, in that special kind of "seeing" that, as Pieper puts it, is directed to more than "the tangible surface of reality." This kind of seeing, Pieper further observes, must be "guided by love" – as the ancient mystics put it, *ubi amor, ibi oculus* (roughly, "where there is love, there is seeing").[14]

Craig Dykstra has used the same themes of seeing and loving in his expla-

nation of what should go into the "formation of character" in Christian higher education. We must work, he says, to shape persons "who see deeply into
the reality of things and who love that reality – over time and across circumstances."[15] And the philosopher Albert Borgmann, a practicing Catholic, also
urges us, in a time when so much scholarship limits itself, he says, to the *sur-
faces* of reality, to rediscover "the eloquence of things" in their particularity, so
as to find "the depth of the world."[16]

We serve a God who cares about the depths – and the breadth and the
heights – of the reality that he has created: "The earth is the Lord's and all that
is in it, the world, and those who live in it" (Psalm 24:1 NRSV). We scholars
study various aspects of that world, and we must do it in the awareness that
what we focus on is indeed a part of the fullness of a created reality that we
are also called to love – and in loving to *see*, to behold, so that we can make
connections and cultivate a proper sense of awe and mystery in the presence
of the depths of created being.

As the events of these past few weeks have made all too obvious, the world
desperately needs lovers of created reality, people who look deeply into the
fullness, and especially – but of course not exclusively – into the complex created fullness that is displayed in human beings, "all who live in it," in all of
their marvelous diversity. To love reality in its depths means that we cannot
help but grieve over the brokenness and woundedness of God's world in its
present condition. And we know that to do so is to share in the sorrows that
reside in the deep places of God's own being. As Abraham Kuyper reminded
us, to abuse human beings who are created in God's image "is to defy the love
of the Maker for His handiwork, willfully giving offense, and grieving the
Maker in that about which His heart is most sensitive."[17]

A central reason we have gathered here is to discuss the big questions
about the aims and purposes of Christian scholarship. We all know that there
have been many in the Christian tradition that have emphasized the importance of pursuing scholarship for its own sake, while others have argued pas-
sionately for a scholarship that speaks directly to the urgent issues of the
human condition. My own sense is that, properly understood, this is a false
dilemma. When C.S. Lewis preached his marvelous 1939 sermon, "Learning
in War-Time,"[18] he acknowledged to his hearers, students who were struggling with the question of what sense it made to continue their studies while
many of their fellow citizens were dying in the struggle against the Nazi curse,
that academic activity can certainly be a way of diverting our attention from
the tragedies that are going on around us. But it can also be, he insisted, an
exercise in faithful discipleship. We Christians can keep at the tasks of studying and teaching because we want to honor the purposes of the God who calls
us to take the deep tragedies of our sinful condition seriously. In the ongoing
cosmic struggle between righteousness and unrighteousness, of which our

recent tragedies are just one very horrifying manifestation, faithful Christian scholarship – a sustained and disciplined seeing that is guided by a love of created reality – can be an important means for promoting the cause of righteousness.

During my scholarly career, I have devoted a lot of my own attention to examining various understandings of Christian involvement in public life; and, not surprisingly, I have rather consistently made a point of praising the Calvinist understanding of such matters. But in the past ten years, while not forsaking my Calvinist convictions, I have felt compelled to acknowledge the need for a modest Lutheran corrective to any thoroughgoing Calvinism. The need for doing this was impressed upon me when I agreed to write a review, for a secular philosophy journal, of Harro Höpfl's reader, published in the Cambridge series, Texts in the History of Political Thought, on Luther and Calvin. As I directly compared the political writings of the two Reformers, I was struck by the irony that Calvin, who is well-known for his emphasis on the ravages of sin in human affairs, showed a surprising lack of sensitivity to the tragic dimensions of politics. Here Luther actually seemed to be the better Calvinist. In his wonderful essay "On Secular Authority," Luther warns that the Christian prince must be ever vigilant if he wants his public service to be pleasing to the Lord. And even when the prince does all that he can to promote the cause of righteousness, Luther quickly adds, he should fully expect that he "will soon feel the cross lying on his neck."[19]

Luther's counsel applies also to our work as Christian scholars. We cannot avoid the weight of the Cross as we attempt to fulfill our callings. For some of us the Cross's pressure on our necks will mean that we have to keep at our "ordinary" research and teaching projects even as our television screens replay, over and over again, horrible scenes of human suffering. For others it will mean that we must fight the temptation to pursue the ordinary, as we revise our scholarly plans in order to address more directly the ongoing crises. This is why we need Christian scholarly networks, communities where the spiritual gifts are nurtured, so that we can assist each other as we seek to discern the promptings of the Spirit for our individual and collective scholarly pursuits, as folks who encourage each other to pray, on our own behalf as well as for the sake of a world in crisis:

> Just as I am, though tossed about,
> with many a conflict, many a doubt,
> fightings and fears, within, without,
> O Lamb of God, I come.[20]

And as people who hold on for dear life to the Savior's promise, even as it speaks to our academic endeavors: "Take my yoke upon you, and learn from me; for I am gentle and humble in heart…. [M]y yoke is easy, and my burden is light" (Matthew 11: 29-30 NRSV). By God's grace, may we find it to be so.

---

[1] Michael D. Cohen and James G. March, *Leadership and Ambiguity: The American College President* (New York: McGraw-Hill Book Company, 1974), 195.

[2] Charlotte Elliott, "Just as I Am, without One Plea," 1836.

[3] Frank E. Gaebelein, *The Christian, The Arts, And Truth: Regaining The Vision Of Greatness*, ed. D. Bruce Lockerbie (Portland, Oregon: Multnomah Press, 1985), 154-155.

[4] Alasdair MacIntyre, *After Virtue: A Study in Moral Theory* (Notre Dame, IN: University of Notre Dame Press, 1984), 68.

[5] Michael A. Hakkenberg, "The Battle over the Ordination of Gordon H. Clark, 1943-1948," in *Pressing Toward the Mark: Essays Commemorating Fifty Years of the Orthodox Presbyterian Church*, ed. Charles G. Dennison and Richard C. Gamble (Philadelphia: The Committee for the Historian of the Orthodox Presbyterian Church, 1986), 329-350.

[6] Edward John Carnell to Harold John Ockenga, 10 October 1954, in the collection of the Ockenga Institute, Gordon-Conwell Theological Seminary.

[7] Monika K. Hellwig, "The Survival of Catholic Higher Education," *America*, 16-23 July 2001, 23.

[8] Hellwig, 24.

[9] Hellwig, 24.

[10] Mark A. Noll, *The Scandal of the Evangelical Mind* (Grand Rapids: Wm. B. Eerdmans, 1994).

[11] George Marsden, *The Outrageous Idea of Christian Scholarship* (New York: Oxford University Press, 1997).

[12] Jeffrey Stout, *Ethics after Babel: The Languages of Morals and their Discontents* (Boston: Beacon Press, 1988), 74.

[13] Nicholas Wolterstorff, *Reason Within the Bounds of Religion* (Grand Rapids: Wm. B. Eerdmans, 1976), 59-66, esp. 66.

[14] Josef Pieper, *Only the Lover Sings: Art and Contemplation*, trans. Lothar Krauth (San Francisco: Ignatius Press, 1990), 72-74.

[15] Craig Dykstra, "Communities of Conviction and the Liberal Arts," *The Council of Societies for the Study of Religion Bulletin* 19, no. 3 (1990): 62. Dykstra makes this case in greater detail in his *Vision and Character: A Christian Educator's Alternative to Kohlberg* (New York: Paulist Press, 1981).

[16] Albert Borgmann, *Crossing the Postmodern Divide* (Chicago: The University of Chicago Press, 1992), 51, 106.

[17] Abraham Kuyper, *To Be Near Unto God*, trans. John Hendrik de Vries (1925; reprint, Grand Rapids: Baker Book House, 1979), 30-31.

[18] C.S. Lewis, *The Weight of Glory and Other Addresses* (Grand Rapids: Wm. B. Eerdmans, 1965), 43-54.

[19] Harro Höpfl, ed., trans., *Luther and Calvin on Secular Authority*, Cambridge Texts in the History of Political Thought (Cambridge: Cambridge University Press, 1991), 41.

[20] Charlotte Elliott, "Just as I Am, without One Plea," 1836.

Christian Scholarship for Whom?

Elizabeth Conde-Frazier

John Calvin wrote, "Doctrine is not an affair of the tongue but of the life."[1] The same might be said of Christian scholarship.

As scholars, many of us have been drawn to our work because of the passion that is in us. That passion has been shaped by who we are, by our life journeys, by the experiences that we have had. Last summer my colleagues and I worked with a group of about fifty young people, and what we did first was to help them find their passion. These young people brought in music videos and CDs, they walked through their neighborhood, they looked at newspaper clippings and listened to the news, and they had wonderful conversations with each other as they began to identify some common passions – things that made them joyful or made them angry about the world. And from those common passions they then started to do research.

For example, I worked with a group of young people who were looking at the entertainment industry and the messages that industry puts out to young people. They critiqued the music they listened to and the accompanying music videos. They invited people from the music industry, financial advisors as well as pop singers, and they asked them some penetrating questions. They were trying to understand how the whole thing worked together. It was fabulous to see their minds ticking. After their research, they did some dreaming about how the music industry could change. Then they focused on a couple of things that they could do to change it.

They found their passion – to love God with all your soul. They did research – to love God with all your mind. They did the dreaming – to love God with all your heart. But they also did the action – to love God with all your strength.

"Christian scholarship for whom?" cannot be answered unless we have a visual inner image of the "whom." So, when I ask myself "Scholarship for whom?" I think of Jose Escamilla, a pastor in San Diego whose parishioners are people who come across the border everyday. I think of Jeremiah, who was taught that he was stupid because everyday someone told him he was stupid. When he came to my class, he said, "You know I am stupid, but God called me so that's why I'm here. Be patient with me." I sat with Jeremiah, and I found that he had not been taught the essentials of reading: how to comprehend, how to infer. But when I taught him those things, he found out how brilliant he was and his excitement was contagious. I think of Judy Herbert whose work as a religious educator is with women who have been incarcerated and are trying to start their lives again. Judy sees me, a scholar, as a resource to her in her work with these women.

Who are the faces in your scholarly world? The people with names, not categories of people. Who are the faces that connect with your research? As we begin to think about "Christian scholarship for whom?" situate yourself with God in the world and see the people, see the faces, know the names of your neighbor.

Scholarship in the Service of God's Reign

In his book, *Moral Man and Immoral Society,* Reinhold Niebuhr claims that reason, to some degree, will always be a servant of self-interest.[2] Our scholarly interests, for example, are often in the service of the academy and our institutions as well as our concerns for personal promotion within these institutions. Reinhold Niebuhr recognized the limits of reason because of this self-interest and therefore realized that reason alone cannot move us to ethical attitudes. Instead, he argued, personal intimate and organic contacts are needed. Rational persuasion is not enough to bring about social justice. Believing this about the nature of humanity, Niebuhr came to the conclusion that the dilemma of overcoming self-interest must be approached with the humility of knowing that the reign of God is impossible to realize except by God's grace. It is indeed in that spirit that I, along with you, approach the task of a dialogue with you about Christian scholarship for whom.

I want to suggest that our research, our scholarship, is in the service of God's reign and that God's reign is a reign of love and of social justice. This understanding therefore re-shapes our scholarship and brings to it questions such as these:

- How do we seriously take into consideration our position of power as researchers?
- How does the very process of our research provide the opportunity for others to empower themselves?
- How do we take into consideration the questions and interests which our "subjects" have rather than concentrating merely on our own? Is there a methodology that facilitates the divestment of our own questions?

These questions are important to us as Christian scholars because the knowledge generated by scholars oftentimes defines the codes of knowledge that form the basis of organizational life in our society, such as schools, hospitals, clinics, the military, business and religious life. The professional elite of these organizations (administrators, researchers, teachers, social workers, doctors, nurses, youth workers, and ministers, to name a few) define the knowledge of discourse and thus build the framework of meaning about how the organization operates.

These factors imply that the knowledge generated by our scholarship has the power to control the daily life, and therefore the quality of life, of persons. To break this control, postmodern philosophers and social theorists such as Roberto Unger, Andreas Huyssen and Cornel West have advocated that scholars be educated by struggling peoples.[3] This stance reflects a shift in the focus of scholarship away from the "search for foundations and the quest for certainty" toward more utilitarian approaches to the production of knowledge.[4]

Cornel West suggests that intellectual activity or scholarship should foster methods for examining the everyday life so that, through critical reflection and social action, a more creative democracy will be encouraged. He advocates ways of living and working together that foster greater participation in activities affecting our daily lives. He urges persons in the academic and professional life of the communities to give up "on the search for foundations and the quest for certainty," and to shift their energies to defining "the social and communal circumstances under which persons can communicate and cooperate in the process of acquiring knowledge."[5] West asserts the need for the scholarly community to be in solidarity with "the wretched of the earth," so that as we educate and are educated by this community of persons, we might come to relate the life of the mind to the collective life of the community.

Truth Seeking and Solidarity with the Poor

As Christian scholars, however, we need not give up our search for the foundations of truth in order to be in solidarity with the poor and marginalized. Truth for us is revealed in Jesus Christ, not in a metaphysical ideal. Jesus, the Incarnate One, represents the physical human reality. Jesus is incarnated in that reality, and Paul reminds the Corinthians that wisdom is found both in the foolishness of this incarnation and in the crucifixion. God also discloses God's will and purpose to the poor, weak, and dispossessed (1 Corinthians 1:18-31). If we believe this, then we realize the importance of dialogue and solidarity with the poor and marginalized.[6]

Let us bring these arguments into greater theological perspective by looking at knowledge and the inquiry for knowledge as it relates to the incarnation and to truth as revelation. How we understand the nature of God's revelation in scripture is important. If, for example, the revelation or truth about

God is propositional, then it is a truth divorced from existential concretion, or the concrete realities of persons. It elevates the cognitive dimensions and bifurcates it from the affective. Theologian Samuel Solivan cautions that this movement dehumanizes the revelation.[7]

In propositional revelation, the questions and answers are stated by someone outside the context of particular communities. It reduces the possibilities of our inquiry. It neglects to ask what Paul meant when he stated in the Corinthian letter that God discloses God's will and purpose to the poor, weak, and dispossessed. When, however, the knowledge or truth revealed to the non-scholarly community and that of the scholarly is shared, the Holy Spirit brings to light truths that had not been evident until that moment of engagement.

Orthopathos, Pneumatology, and Incarnation

To capture this dynamic and to address West's philosophical concerns as Christians, we may look to a theology of *orthopathos*. Orthopathos makes use of the two terms "ortho" and "pathos." "Ortho" means straight, upright; "pathos," in the classical Greek understanding, refers to self-alienation. Generally it refers to the experience of suffering or anguish that can result in self-alienation. In the early Christian tradition, the understanding of pathos was self-empowering, particularly as presented in the climax of the Christian message where God is the one who loves to the point of suffering. The term "orthopathos" makes the distinction between suffering that results in self-alienation and suffering that becomes a source for liberation and social transformation. It is looking for a way to transform human suffering into a resource for liberation.[8]

Orthopathos, then, is doing theology by engaging with those who suffer. Solivan calls this a "conjunctive theological method."[9] It bridges the "truth claims made by orthodoxy and the liberating engagement sought by orthopraxis."[10] As such, Solivan presents orthopathos as a way to "appropriate pathos," or suffering, "as an epistemological resource."[11] In other words, our way of knowing is to enter into the world of those who struggle. It is in this struggle that we encounter new truth. We come to this truth through the guidance of the Holy Spirit, and it is a truth that redeems.

The affirmation of our pneumatology in our scholarship gives it an orthodox starting point. The Holy Spirit is given to the church for its work and function; it gives the church the capacity for knowledge since it leads us into all truth (John 16:13). This affirmation provides the foundation for us to allow the Spirit to lead us into truth in our scholarship, if we see our vocation as the work of the Holy Spirit in the church and the world. The Spirit leading us into all truth requires that the truth continue to unfold before us and brings prophecy and hope. (We will say more about scholarship as prophecy a bit later.) In the light of this, we must take contextualization seriously. Who we are and the world of which we are a part become a fundamental basis for Christian critical scholarship.

The incarnation gives us the theological framework for contextualization. In incarnation, God becomes human. God identifies with us so that God can become personally present and real to us in an unprecedented manner. Jesus has made God contextual. In Jesus, God becomes radically related to humanity in new ways. God relates to the harsh realities of those who are hurt, oppressed, and destitute. "Jesus the Christ, the incarnate son of God, is the touchstone that informs the existential realities of the suffering poor."[12] The incarnation is the dwelling or "tabernacling" of God among us, and it grounds Jesus' mission among us as one of love. It is God's self-giving even to the point of sacrifice. This sacrifice begins when God takes the form of humanity, renouncing heavenly status, and becoming a slave. It is extended into death on the cross (Philippians 2:5-11). Emptying himself was voluntary self-impoverishment. Its purpose was to bring new possibility of life for humanity and all of creation. To follow the spirit of the kenosis is to see our scholarship as servanthood.

It is in the person of Jesus that we can discern the mode of operation of the universe. The gospel of John captures this understanding through the use of the word *logos*. Logos was a word widely used in religion and philosophy long before John wrote his gospel. In the Greek it signifies both reason and spoken word, encompassing the inner thought and outward expression. Jesus' words were spirit and life, and his signs were the outward expression of the presence and power of God. In Jesus, the logos is both reason and flesh. Christian scholarship must reflect both dimensions, and therefore must be relational. Throughout the gospel, John shows us the effect of the incarnation, which is enlightenment (John 1:5,9) and life (John 3:15).

Finally, the incarnation means that the mediating principle between God and the world is no longer an idea, a philosophical term, but a human life. In our research, this transforms the mediating principle between myself and the persons whom I wish to know better. It signifies that the purpose for which our relationship is formed is also transformed. No longer are we researcher and subjects but persons in a mutual agreement or covenant, if you will, who engage together in the study of a common interest. This covenant divests me of power as the researcher and makes the participants equal to me. One of the goals of this common study is edification or empowerment.

In *To Know As We Are Known,* Parker Palmer captures the issues of incarnational research as he speaks about two lines of sight: that of fact and reason, and that of the heart, so that we may see "one world, in all its dimensions, healed and made whole."[13] Without each one of these dimensions, the other by itself is a "diminishment of reality."[14] He goes on to point out the problem of knowledge that emerges as "we impose a mental order on the chaos that surrounds us," and of the ways in which we use "concepts to organize our impressions and theories to organize our concepts."[15] This knowledge of fact and reason, he says, reduces truth to what makes us win and to what moves us into and up the ladder of professional academic life. This is a process that distances or alienates us from the world around us, turning persons into pawns in our game of winning.[16] This manner of knowing, he states, "begins and ends in human pride and power."[17]

Knowledge is Relational

In contrast, knowledge in the biblical sense is relational. Knowledge in the Hebrew Scriptures means to know in the realistic sense, referring to persons and things with which we are familiar. To know in this way implies a personal relationship between the knower and the person known. It is to know from experience, to know, for example, afflictions, loss of children, disease or grief. *Yada*, or to know, in the Hebrew can also be used to designate sexual intercourse. This usage points to the fact that for the Hebrew to know implies the specific relationship in which the individual stands with the one who is known.

Knowledge is an activity in which the totality of one's being is engaged, not only the mind. We can derive from this that knowledge is always accompanied by an emotional response. Full comprehension is manifested in action that corresponds to the relationship apprehended. In the prophetic writings, Israel's lack of knowledge is not theoretical ignorance but the failure to practice the filial or devoted relationship in which they stand with God.[18]

The initial encounter with the one to be known does not yield immediate, full, and true knowledge. To know God comes from knowing God in the historical events in which God has evidenced or is showing God's interest in humanity. It is, therefore, knowing God in the biblical text as well as in the everyday historical events of life. This everyday reality of life is named *lo cotidiano* by Hispanic theologians. It is the experience of the transcendent in the immanent. It "allows us to see how . . . God's grace, justice, and love are manifest in everyday occurrences."[19] Theologian Loida Martell-Otero points out that *lo cotidiano* allows "the voiceless to tell their stories," and to "cry out to the heavens for justice and peace."[20]

We come to know God through the witness of others, and this witness urges or inspires us to seek God for ourselves. Teaching that guides persons to seek God leads them to knowledge that, in turn, makes them ready to live the kind of life that allows God to teach them further. Teaching takes the experiences through which we pass and makes us aware of God in them; the transcendent is revealed in the immanent. Finally, our knowledge of God implies knowledge of ourselves in relation to God, so that we assume our religious obligations. In the Scriptures, the grammatical object of "to know" is frequently God's ways or precepts, not just God (Psalm 25:4,12; 119:104). It is knowing the experience of the reality of God and not the propositions concerning God.

In the New Testament, the realization of God's redemptive work modifies what it is to know God, thus bringing it to new levels. The subject matter of knowledge is the mystery of the kingdom of God. To know God is to know the will of God through God's redemptive purpose. This knowledge leads to a harmony of wills.

Finally, in Johannine literature, to know God is to love the neighbor. Notice that the Scriptures do not give the term "other" to persons in our midst, a term that already reflects alienation between us. The gospel message makes it clear that the "other," the Samaritan, the Syrophoenecian woman, the centurion, the lepers are neighbors. Today the Latina, the African American, the Afghans, the gay and the lesbian, the Vietnamese, the Palestinian, and the illegal alien are our neighbors, not the "other." To know God is to love my neighbor.

Scholarship in the service of the kingdom of God brings me to the knowledge of God through the knowledge of my neighbor. This is scholarship with the purpose of constructing or building up the community. It is scholarship motivated by "neighbor consciousness." This consciousness leads us to social justice, an integral dimension of the spiritual life. It is the Holy Spirit who empowers humanity into the fullness of relational life. It is through the Holy Spirit that the grace Niebuhr deemed necessary will be made available. To speak of "scholarship for whom," and to place this discussion in the theological/biblical framework of relational knowledge, is to place our questions about scholarship within the realm of social justice.

Christian Scholarship as Social Justice: Participatory Action Research

Justice is a struggle for human dignity. Gustavo Gutiérrez defines justice by speaking of the God of life who is revealed to us in Jesus. He states: "The lack of the necessities for living a human life is contrary to the will of God.... A profession of faith in that God implies a rejection of this inhuman situation."[21] Walter Brueggemann speaks of *shalom*. Shalom is a broader vision that encompasses justice. He points out that "The central vision of world history in the Bible is that all of creation is one, every creature in community with every other, living in harmony and security toward the joy and well-being of every other creature."[22] This vision includes not only human creatures but also every living thing, encompassing all of the earth. Shalom is a vision of connectedness, not a vision for individuals but for the whole community – young, old, rich, poor, powerful, and dependent. It "is the outgrowth of a covenant... in which persons are bound not only to God but to one another."[23]

These definitions give shape to what it means to do scholarship that moves us toward social justice. One must also bring context, history, and culture to the dynamic of inquiry, as well as economic and political realities, with the purpose of seeing how these mitigate against the full humanity and dignity of self and others. Let us take a look at scholarship that seeks to embody social justice in the ways we have been discussing.

Participatory action research (PAR) is an umbrella term that includes several traditions of theory and practice. Participation recognizes that including practitioners, community members, citizens, employees, and volunteers is essential to the generation of useful knowledge regarding major social, political, economic, technical, cultural, and organizational problems. The knowledge comes from the people. Action indicates that the research is intended to contribute directly to the efforts of the participants. Research indicates a systemic effort to generate knowledge. It may include historical, literary, theological, and scientific forms. The major thrust is to focus the knowledge generated on changes that improve the quality of living. It is research that is attached to the humanization of persons in communities. Unattached research tends to create policies that continue to oppress. In summary, let us say that we have a problem in a specific community. That community, in collaboration with trained researchers, will collect and analyze information, and in taking action will improve or solve their problem.

The resources and energy needed to sustain such a process of reflection, analysis, and action calls for a network of institutions to come together. Consider the following example of PAR in a church.

A church asked a theological school to partner with them to collect some data on a problem they had identified in the community. This was done in dialogue so that the congregation still provided most of the understanding of how the community worked, while the theological students helped design an organized way to collect and process the data. Dependence was avoided as the students apprenticed the church leaders for their future work. The students helped the church do pastoral visits in their community, a model to which deacons and others in the church who did visitation could relate. This method used the church's skills and insights while teaching members to design questions that focused specifically on the issues they wished to investigate. The entire process was grounded in the theology of the mission of the church, namely a commitment to serve the everyday lives of the people of the community.

The church members also learned how to categorize and analyze the information as a group. They looked at interconnected institutions and began to piece together an understanding of the systemic issues and how these were constructed. Working as groups, instead of calling in a consultant, was very productive. The youth became involved because in this Hispanic community they could manage the English language better than the adults. It was the young people who mapped out ways to eliminate the redundant procedures institutions forced upon their clients, and it was they who designed the strategies for advocacy.

During this process, the community and the church were learning to become neighbors. People would drop in and update information and give names of helpful contact persons at various institutions. When the church contacted these persons, they learned the ins and outs of social services and the frustrations with which the caseworkers dealt. Slowly (the whole process took five years), many who were in the system trying to make a difference began to connect with each other through the church. It was as if the church had become the switchboard. Trust and mutuality were built as persons learned from each other and connected the knowledge they all had in order to design better strategies for serving the community.

At times, the students wanted to move immediately into action, but the church leaders reminded them that change doesn't take place in a church without founding it on theological reflection based on the witness of God in their daily struggles and the Scriptures. Now it was their turn to apprentice the students. The Scriptures were a source of knowledge that guided the congregation in the knowledge of God's love for their neighbor. God so loved the world that God became flesh and entered into the reality of persons by becoming present in the world to transform it. The congregation reflected on what it would mean to follow this example as a model for their ministry in the community.

Conversations on spirituality with church members were sought by professionals on their own terms as they struggled through the long process of moving from a sense of powerlessness to empowerment, while carrying out their vocations in the midst of unjust structures. The church responded by making their building available for prayer and meditation, holding healing services for patients, their families, and service providers. The church also held meetings to talk about strategies, followed by what was termed by those in attendance as "justice rituals." Many new symbols emerged from these rituals, which were composed by a community of professionals participating together in a process of struggling to make their faith meaningful.

The theological school, by invitation of the church, became involved in the process as needed. Many students did their contextualized internships in that setting. They learned much about creating and maintaining community, about the model of the church as neighbor, and about the ways to restructure church programming so that the habits and spiritual formation of the faith community would be consistent with kingdom values. This was a process of constant reflection, with worship reflecting the changes of the community's efforts to live faithfully.

The school found that the pastors and laypersons were partners in the teaching not only at the church but in the classroom as well. They became speakers and panelists for many classes. The church found that the reflection students brought to the congregation through Bible study, healing services, and justice rituals were invigorating. The students found that what they studied at the school was not so alien to the church or community context after all.

In this process, the community's interests are defined and made central rather than the researcher's. The researcher stands alongside the community and not outside as an objective observer or external consultant. The researcher's role is that of facilitator and/or catalyst. The researcher enables persons to analyze their situation and to change what they want. The researcher helps to locate resources and to analyze issues. In this example, knowledge acquisition was a collective process that emerged from those who were attempting to improve their quality of life. As the process took place, it was those who were struggling with the issues that defined the body of understanding on which community life would be based.

Traditional research usually ends up in a journal or a book. Incarnational research provides the tools for solving problems experienced by the people in communities, though one can also write about the process. The purpose, however, is to make a difference by engaging persons directly affected by the problem to formulate their own solutions.

Incarnational research is disciplined inquiry that focuses its efforts "to improve the quality of people's organizational, community and family lives."[24] It uses a hermeneutic and dialogical or meaning-making approach that is more democratic, humanizing, empowering, and life enhancing.[25]

This is inquiry that collects data, analyzes it, theorizes, and comes to action as a result. The action begins in the process of the inquiry, as it requires us to develop relationships among persons for group participation. This is not a linear approach to research but an organic one that takes into account the social, cultural, and emotional factors that affect human activity. It is scholarship that fosters trust and mutual understanding.

We evaluate our research by asking what impact it has on the daily lives of persons. Scholarship is not only about the knowledge generated but about who controls that knowledge and to whom it is made accessible. In whose service are the questions formed? Who is left out? How is the knowledge that it generates affected because of the sources not acknowledged? Why is it that such sources are not deemed valuable and viable? How does not valuing such sources affect others? What are the policies and structures that are put into place as a result of the *whom* of our scholarship? Are these policies liberating and hopeful or are they oppressive and dehumanizing?

Christian Scholarship as Prophetic Scholarship

This type of research yields truth that takes form in us. That form is devotion. Devotion is the act or condition of giving oneself up for another person, purpose, or service. It is setting ourselves apart for this type of deep, steady affection as our spiritual worship.

Devotion as a part of our scholarship makes it prophetic scholarship. In the Hebrew Scriptures, one of the functions of the prophet was to convey to those who would believe the divinely imparted meaning of history.[26] Prophets or seers exercised the function of seeing or of intellectually grasping that which is not normally accessible. They spoke forth and announced it so that understanding or knowledge was made available to all who heard the proclamation. To see is to announce. Note the importance of the intellect for apprehending both the way of God and the meaning of our times. Also note that what we grasp is not normally accessible, and our task is to announce it in ways that can be attained by others. This means we must have an awareness of how people learn and of appropriate teaching methodologies.

The prophet mulls over, reflects upon, and wrestles with the word. This process involves the best rational powers of the prophet because she/he must determine how, in what context, when, for whom, and in what way most effectively to deliver the word of judgement. The prophet's vocation is to open people's hearts, to enhance their understanding, and to bring about their turning back to God. This is transformational learning.

The seer not only conveys but reveals. The revelation is of the invisible God and of people visible to God but made invisible to others by injustices. To reveal these injustices is to reveal those who live under the weight of them. God and the people who are invisible become apprehensible and audible. This gift is practiced through a combination of skills particular to each prophet, but the prophet is also guided, moved, or restrained by God.

The prophet understands the passion of God in the present moment and evokes passion in others. To impassion others is to be stirred in one's own soul. The passion comes from an understanding of and fellowship with the feelings of God, or a communion with the divine consciousness. This communion takes place not only through prayer but also through our fellowship with our neighbor. The passion comes from reflection upon or participation in the divine pathos where God is involved in the life of the community. We have divine consciousness and neighbor consciousness engaging each other.

This is what Abraham Heschel calls sympathy with God or feeling the feelings of God.[27] The burden of a prophet is compassion for humanity and sympathy with God. It is no wonder then that, while a philosopher indulges in the metaphysical discourses of being and becoming, of matter and form, the wide spaces opened through the elegance of the mind, a prophet is concerned with single mothers, corrupt police departments, and market affairs. The prophet rants and raves "as if the whole world were a slum." What for many may be trivial or a single and slight isolated act, for the prophet is a disaster, "a deathblow to existence."[28]

Prophecy is living in the borderland between God and the people. The prophet learns to observe, to collect data, to analyze or make meaning from the data, and to synthesize it in order to come up with insight and action. Insight is wisdom or understanding from the inside in dealing with facts or people. It is the power to see deeply, to penetrate, and to see distinctions and relations. Critical thinking is making connections and seeing implications. Imagination is for looking at what form to give to the wisdom we have derived. How does it shape the world differently? Action comes as we organize our thinking to see the causes of reality. Our actions are then informed by this critical reflection. In liberation theology this is known as *praxis.*

The prophet also senses God's feelings. Feelings are important because they mediate relationships not only between persons but also between subjects. Relationship between subjects is important because when we separate everyday reality, *lo cotidiano,* from theory, we create possibilities for oppressing others.

God's feelings are for those who are plundered of the profound riches of the world. They are feelings that a prophet feels not through some mystic inspiration but because he/she is involved with the people. The prophet's own life and soul are at stake in what is announced and denounced.

How does a prophet live in this borderland where she can both pray for mercy when God calls for judgement while also identifying with God's threat of punishment or wrath? How can the prophet live out this tension and paradox of compassion for the people and sympathy with God? Heschel suggests that intimacy with God is the answer.[29] This intimacy is illustrated through the words of Amos:

> Do two walk together unless they have made an appointment?…
> Surely the Lord God does nothing, without revealing his secret to his
> servants the prophets. (Amos 3:3,7 New Revised Standard Version).

God's heart and mind are open to the prophet to such a degree that they come to know and understand one another deeply. The prophet walks with both the people and with God in an intimacy that shapes her servanthood to both.

To walk with the people is to be in solidarity. For Gustavo Gutiérrez, solidarity does not begin in the rhetoric of social justice nor in the occasional visits with the poor. It begins with a conversion or "turning to." In *Beber en su propio pozo,* Gutiérrez defines conversion as a point of departure for a spiritual pathway, a break with the life that we have had up to this point so that we might start a new way. [30] He describes this new life through the Lukan passage: "Sell all that you own… then come, follow me" (Luke 18:22 NRSV). Gutiérrez states:

Without this second aspect the breaking away would lack the horizontal dimension and certainly it would lack sense....

This is why conversion is not a gesture that is realized once and for all. It implies a development, even a painful one, for uncertainty, doubt, and the temptation to unwalk what we have walked are never absent.[31]

Conclusion

To summarize, allow me to bring to our recollection the words of Paul in 1 Corinthians 2:4-5. Paul said, "My speech and my proclamation were not with plausible words of wisdom, but with a demonstration of the Spirit and of power" (NRSV). The Spirit and power of God are love for "God is love" (1 John 4:8). Devotion is the demonstration of the Spirit and of power. It points to the who of our scholarship, re-shaping it and the institutions and structures that foster and promote Christian scholarship.

Our present criteria for excellent scholarship is limiting to incarnational research. It does not, for example, have ways of giving consideration to and rewarding the scholar's life of engagement with a community. It obligates one to limit the quest for knowledge to the realms of the library or to empirical study alone. Tenure, the symbol of scholarly excellence, means that one has published. Published for whom? Who has access to it, other scholars? How has it impacted the life of the community beyond the scholarly community? Does it reflect relational knowledge in the biblical sense?

The demonstration of the Spirit and of power takes place when our scholarship contributes to the healing places of disconnection or alienation of one from the other. It is scholarship that emerges from our embrace of both the pain and the pathos of the oppressed and the promise of the reign of love and justice. This is scholarship in service to the ministry of reconciliation.

Brueggemann reminds us that when we fail to yield to the gift of the Spirit, the Spirit does not come among us.[32] My desire is that our Christian scholarship will be servant and prophetic scholarship for social justice to the poor and marginalized, that it will facilitate a space for attentiveness to the Spirit in the daily lives of persons, and that it will invite "Come, Holy Spirit, come!"

---

[1] John Calvin, *Institutes of the Christian Religion*, trans. Henry Beveridge, 2 vols. (London: James Clarke & Co., 1949), III.vi.4. Cited in Sara Little, *To Set One's Heart: Belief and Teaching in the Church* (Atlanta: John Knox Press, 1983), 20.

[2] See Reinhold Niebuhr, *Moral Man and Immoral Society: A Study in Ethics and Politics* (New York: Charles Scribner's Sons, 1932).

[3] See Roberto Mangabeira Unger, *Social Theory: Its Situation and Its Task: A Critical Introduction to "Politics, A Work in Constructive Social Theory"* (Cambridge: Cambridge University Press, 1987); Andreas Huyssen, *After the Great Divide: Modernism, Mass Culture, Postmodernism*, Theories of Representation and Difference (Bloomington: Indiana University Press, 1986); and Cornel West, *The American Evasion of Philosophy: A Genealogy of Pragmatism*, The Wisconsin Project on American Writers (Madison: The University of Wisconsin Press, 1989).

[4] West, 213.

[5] West, 213.

[6] See Samuel Solivan, "Orthopathos: Prolegomenon for a North American Hispanic Theology" (Ph.D. diss., Union Theological Seminary, 1993), 96.

[7] Solivan, "Orthopathos," 96-97. See also Samuel Solivan, *The Spirit, Pathos and Liberation: Toward an Hispanic Pentecostal Theology* (Sheffield: Sheffield Academic Press, 1998).

[8] Solivan, "Orthopathos," 91-92.

[9] Solivan, "Orthopathos," 103.

[10] Solivan, "Orthopathos," 104.

[11] Solivan, "Orthopathos," 91.

[12] Solivan, "Orthopathos," 126.

[13] Parker J. Palmer, *To Know As We Are Known: A Spirituality of Education* (San Francisco: Harper & Row, 1983), xi.

[14] Palmer, xii.

[15] Palmer, 3.

[16] Palmer, 3-4.

[17] Palmer, 5.

[18] Insights gathered from *The Interpreter's Dictionary of the Bible: An Illustrated Encyclopedia*, s.v. "Knowledge."

[19] Loida I. Martell-Otero, "*Lo Cotidiano:* Finding God in the spaces of the everyday," *The Witness* 83, no. 12 (2000): 21.

[20] Martell-Otero, 21.

[21] Gustavo Gutiérrez, *The God of Life,* trans. Matthew J. O'Connell (Maryknoll, NY: Orbis Books, 1991), xi.

[22] Walter Brueggemann, *Living Toward a Vision: Biblical Reflections on Shalom* (Philadelphia: United Church Press, 1976), 15. Shalom is a concept that cannot be captured by a single word, for it includes many dimensions: love, loyalty, truth, grace, salvation, justice, blessing, and righteousness.

[23] Brueggemann, 17.

[24] Emily F. Calhoun, "Action research: Three approaches," *Educational Leadership* 51, no. 2 (1993): 62, quoted in Ernest T. Stringer, *Action Research: A Handbook for Practitioners* (Thousand Oaks, CA: Sage Publications, 1996), 9.

[25] Stringer, 9.

[26] In this section, I draw on the insights of B.D. Napier. See *The Interpreter's Dictionary of the Bible,* s.v. "Prophet, Prophetism."

[27] These insights come from Abraham J. Heschel, *The Prophets* (New York: Harper & Row, Publishers, 1962), 26.

[28] Heschel, 3-4.

[29] Heschel, 38.

[30] Gustavo Gutiérrez, *Beber en su propio pozo: En el itinerario espiritual de un pueblo* [We drink from our own wells: the spiritual journey of a people], 4th ed. (Salamanca: Ediciones Sígueme, 1986), 124.

[31] Gutiérrez, *Beber en su propio pozo,* 125. "*Sin este segundo aspecto el rompimiento carecería de horizonte y en definitiva de sentido . . . Por eso mismo la conversión no es un gesto que se realiza una vez por todas. Ella implica un desarrollo, doloroso incluso, en el que no están ausentes las incertidumbres, las dudas, las tentaciones de desandar lo andado.*"

[32] Brueggemann, 149.

Why Christian Scholarship Needs Story and Art

Marilynne Robinson

I am something of an outsider at an event like this. I have read theology, I have studied the Bible, and I have written about both of them, but it has been on the basis of my own interest and research and in the absence of any contact at all with actual, practicing scholars of religion. My sense of the state of things has a variety of sources, none of them trivial, but none of a kind to make me aware of the assumptions and preoccupations of religious scholars in general or in the Reformed tradition, or in this room. What I am aware of are the attitudes and the state of knowledge of my students, the ways scholarship and the Bible tend to be discussed in my church, and the quality of thought and scholarship I find when I look for resources to help me in writing about or teaching the Bible.

So perhaps nothing I say will be in the least germane to anyone here, except in the fact that the world at large is our only real subject and concern. I will argue that Christian scholarship, in the forms in which serious lay people encounter it, is a powerful obstacle to understanding and faith, and that this is true in great part because it refuses to honor the narrative art of Scripture.

Here is an instance. I have used Solomon's prayer at the dedication of the Temple to make the point that the blessing Solomon, in his wisdom, asked of God, was that God would judge Israel, that he would establish justice in Israel, and that he would do so even at great cost to her in pain and sorrow. I wanted to explain to the students the extreme ethical rigor of the historical and prophetic writing, and to make the point that it asserted the attentive presence of God and the felt authority of God, both of which ancient Israel – to its eternal credit – avidly desired. I looked a little way into the scholarship and found that the Deuteronomist had written this speech, some time after the Babylonians burned Solomon's Temple, and he wrote it to shore up the authority of the text and the restored Temple cult. We know the Deuteronomist did it because he is always up to that sort of thing. In his *Theology of the Old Testament*, Walter Brueggemann attributes some elements of the prayer to the Deuteronomist and some to the Priestly tradition, and describes it admiringly as a strategy "to extricate Yahweh from a failed temple system."[1]

This assertion is a challenge to the integrity of the narrative in both senses of the word. There is no reason to suppose that Solomon would not have spoken at an event as momentous as this one, or that his words would not have been recorded, or preserved in memory. And cities were sacked and populations slaughtered and enslaved all over the ancient world. Solomon, or whoever rendered his speech, need not have anticipated the precise event of the destruction of the Temple or the captivity of the people to know such things might well happen. In the same way scholars seem to date the Gospels after 70 CE because Jesus alludes to the pulling down of Herod's Temple, though those big stones that impressed the disciples were so big because the technology for breaching defensive walls had stayed abreast of the technology for building them, and the Romans were the ancient world's greatest engineers. There is nothing implausible in either Jesus' or Solomon's anticipation of these events, nor would there be had they been men of far more modest gifts. The interpretive consequences of these scholarly judgments are enormous in both cases. Solomon's prayer is changed from theology to a contrivance to rationalize a limited and failed theology. I prefer my reading because it resonates with the text. It is an instance of the Bible interpreting the Bible, which, as a powerfully self-referential literature, it is very inclined to do.

This essay has changed considerably from my original intentions for it. My first thought was that I should talk about the way in which fictional narrative supports a complex and humane understanding of human experience almost by its nature, provided only that the writer is committed to giving honest witness. Since consciousness, time, language, human relationship, civilization, history, and the whole great life of non-human nature are expressions of God's will and therefore also expressions of His nature, no one need fear that the exploration of these things will ever lead her away from the practice of art that deserves to be called Christian, provided only that the art is indeed an exploration, made with the fullest integrity. I would have said an obvious thing: that the idea that Christianity is a sort of compartment within a larger reality and that an artist demonstrates religious faith by remaining within that compartment, or by looking out on reality only from its threshold, diminishes and caricatures religion. I would have said also that real art requires real faith, requiring as it does a giving over of the artist to the work of discovery. I probably would have concluded by saying that, to my mind, good art is always religious, because it is moved by wonder. Non-religious art knows exactly what it wants to tell us. And if, in its confidence, it employs Christian themes and images, it remains, all the same, non-religious. The intellectual Pharisee-ism in such displays of assurance persuades many good people that it is better to remain in the ranks of the sinners. Quite a few of them can even quote Scripture to excellent effect on just this point. Bad "Christian" art is possibly destructive and certainly confusing to anyone trying to appraise the state of religious culture, since it leads many good souls, as it were, to pray in their closets. Stanley Hauerwas explained his writing a letter to me by saying, "There are so few Christians in your line of work." My own experience does not confirm this opinion, which I know is very widely held. On the contrary, I find interest in Christianity and respect for it – in its classic, untelevised forms – to be characteristic of writers generally. Often they are intrigued enough by it to know about things the churches have largely abandoned and forgotten, for example theology and the more obscure regions of the Bible – which is to say, the greater part of the Bible.

It is because the Bible is of interest to writers that I am teaching a seminar in the Iowa Writers' Workshop on the Old Testament, to be followed by a seminar on the New Testament in the spring. I am teaching it as a great literature, that is, as a tradition of great literary art. I have done this before, but never with anything like so strong a sense of how much richness it yields when it is approached in this way. In the course of lecturing on Genesis, I began to realize that my thinking about the topic for this lecture, why Christianity needs art and story, had implied to me that Christianity itself was something *other* than art and story. The earth is the Lord's and the fullness thereof, certainly, but it is a complex and unique literature that tells us that this is true, and what it means for us. I teach the Bible on the assumption that to read it otherwise than as a great literature is to misread it very gravely.

Here is a metaphor I have used to explain my approach to my students: If one of those probes we send into deep space looking for signs of intelligent life were to return a massive stream of data and then fall silent, the best minds of earth would be put to work trying to interpret this information. There would be those who said the probe had responded to pulses of radiation from an unknown source, or suffered some sort of bombardment, or that it had sensed ripples in the fabric of space time, or that all these things had happened in combination. Others might say all that was being heard was a malfunction in the device itself, and yet others would argue that some sort of interference had occurred that textured the transmission accidentally, or that there was a malfunction in the devices that received and recorded it. But suppose that the musicians and musicologists who listened to it said, No, that's music. Some might discern in it a sort of primitive chant, taking seeming complexity from faulty transmission of some kind. Others would no doubt accuse the musicians of naively imposing their own acculturated habits of mind on cryptic and exotic data. Then how would the musicians go about proving that what they heard and saw was indeed music? They would look for a complex, self-referential structure. They would look for theme and variation. They would look for irony and allusion. They would look for tradition, innovation, and stylistic evolution. Granting that extra-terrestrial music might have none of these characteristics, if they were found, then the data in which they appeared should surely best be called music. If there is an element of circularity in this reasoning, so is there in all reasoning, since human consciousness exists in a kind of feedback loop of construction and interpretation, and this is no less true when coherence is being discounted than when it is being inferred. The difference matters, because the attention one pays to music is entirely different from the attention one pays to static.

If the meaningfulness of structure and complex variation are denied, then what music contains by way of utterance cannot be heard. The character of the Bible as literary art is far too little attended to. It has seemed the sophisticated thing for a long time to magnify the effects of interference, real or imagined, and to refuse the attempt at comprehension of the kind an art requires in favor of shrewd hypotheses of every sort that would preclude such an attempt.

This is and has been the work of Christian scholarship. The splendor of the Bible as literature makes a powerful demonstration that has been needed to establish the essential truths and to make them live in human memory and imagination. The old Reformers were like the restorers of frescoes, working to expose the art underneath the obscuring patches and accretions. Their confidence in the competence of the individual to encounter the text was surely at least analogous to the awareness – rather forgotten now – that the relation of any viewer to any piece of art can only be unmediated. If the inability to see art as art is barbarism, then a great part of Christian scholarship has been devoted for generations to plain vandalism. How has this happened?

The September 9, 2001 London *Observer* editorialized on a statement by the Catholic Archbishop of Westminster that "Christianity is being 'vanquished' … in Britain," a statement with which the Archbishop of Canterbury agreed. The editorial said, "We congratulate both men on their candour. And while we fully respect the Christianity that many Britons still practise today, we welcome the dramatic change that clerics are belatedly acknowledging."[2] In such an environment – and England is very like the rest of Europe in this regard – it is not hard to see why debunking would be a popular sport. But why does it flourish among the pious in pious America? A much more important question is, what harm have we done to ourselves in obscuring the beauty of what, historically, has been the most present and moving body of art in our culture? Perhaps, in these times, when the need to reflect on fundamental things is universally conceded, Christian scholarship and culture needs to reflect very deeply on itself.

We Americans have always tended to see work, or at least effort, or in any case activity, as good in itself and as an end in itself. Once virtue was its own reward, now work rewards itself. In many ways this is an admirable trait in a people. Much of great value is accomplished. It must be said at the same time that much of very doubtful value is accomplished also, and with as great diligence, resourcefulness, and panache, because, among us, productivity is so meritorious that it has seldom occurred to us to raise questions about the worthiness of the thing produced. It seems we may have arrived together at a moment in which we will want to test the work we do by stricter standards. The churches are full now. God has our attention. As an inevitable consequence, our priorities are re-ordering themselves. For these and for earthlier reasons we will have to ask what, out of the stupendous welter of our busyness, is necessary, what is sustaining.

I see no reason why artists and scholars should not put their own work to the same test. Our education industry and our culture industry are remarkable for sheer output. Like other industries that produce what the economists would call non-essentials, they have been driven by markets, which are themselves driven by trends and fashions. Being American, they are also driven by the compulsion of their professionals to produce simply in order to produce. Scholarship in almost any field is generated in quantities that would swamp the most diligent attention. I take it to be an aspect of the zeal for productivity that styles and methods pass very rapidly through scholarship and the arts, so painters at any given time are doing variations on a few concepts, writers on a few models of reality, scholars on one or two critical or interpretive devices. There appears to be something at work very like the long noted efficiencies of mass production. The individual craftsman need not pause to reflect on the nature of the thing created. She will not be tempted to improvise or ornament, or he to leave some equivalent of a *Johannes fecit.* Much scholarship particularly reads as if its object were the faithful replication of approved methods, and the loyal demonstration of their usefulness in the processing of some cultural datum the industry had to that point overlooked. When Adam Smith – and it was Adam Smith – worried about the alienation of the worker as a consequence of the methods of mass production, he proposed education as a balm if not a cure. History is notorious for keeping a good many jokes up her sleeve, and one of them is surely that education would itself industrialize, and would approximate, in its quiet way, that very alienation. Criticism of the arts, and the writing of history as well, as they are practiced in the academy, have done what they can to rid themselves of the inflection of the human voice, the shaping touch of a particular human maker.

Colleges and universities in America like to believe they have little influence on the culture at large, of which in general they disapprove. But in fact the percentage of the population they credential is vast. They almost uniquely confer what are called qualifications. For all purposes, they control access to status and influence and also to wealth in this country. They educate the educators, every last one. And they educate the painters and composers and the writers, all of whom know the narrative of human life on earth in the way and to the degree that it has been retailed to them in one or another university. From my work with bright and serious graduate students, many of whom come from what are called the best schools, I can tell you that they know very little, that they know they know very little, and that they have no notion how to correct these deficiencies, though, as writers, they feel limited and disabled by them. And if they have learned respect and compassion for any human creature, it is likely to be Friedrich Nietzsche. I was startled to realize how few of them are aware that the word "cynicism" once had negative connotations. It is hardly to be imagined that what they write will not reflect these things.

All this influence, together with the fact that it is not acknowledged by the institutions that exert it, and therefore is not accepted as a responsibility by them, has created a great momentum in the culture in a direction no one I know considers desirable. There is a widely noted evaporation of the sense of meaning. Its absence has been supplied by our late fantasy of a global economy in which the youth of tomorrow will engage all comers in grueling competition. Competition is a word that has strong appeal for us because it implies work with the arbitrary value of contest, work without any specific product or purpose, and, therefore, work without end. It also implies standardization. Competitive work is available to generalized and objective valuation, the kind of thing *Consumer Reports* is good at, rather than to the judgments made of art or of craft. And, as I have said, the language of standardization is everywhere, having especially overrun what were once the humanities. The universities have been recruited, unmurmuring, to accept the role, not as the handmaiden of commerce but as its fostering mother, its alma mater. Now we know, as all good Christians and all moderately sensible people should always have known, that such grandiose human arrangements hang by a thread. Crisis comes, borders close, and we all forget the great global economy that so recently stimulated, justified, or coerced our actions and decisions. If our decision makers had learned any history, they might never have made the strange assumption that economic competition would not lead to war, the assumption on which, it should now be clear, the whole notion of globalization depended. And if they were not university graduates, they would not be doing our thinking for us.

In our time of trouble, people have crowded the houses of worship, turning to the language of meaning God has given us, and that is a very good and heartening thing. It is a long leap to that language and that kind of meaning from the denatured prosing of academic scholarship. The Bible is full of narrative, and it is full of impassioned human voices. How many of us have now recently endorsed the old truth that "[a]ll people are grass. . . . The grass withers, [and] the flower fades" (Isaiah 40:6, 8 New Revised Standard Version) and have taken comfort from the plain truth of it, the deep sorrow of that ancient human utterance?

Well, here I turn to the subject of Christian scholarship, a subject I may be taking a little more literally than the organizers of this conference intended. There is a sense in which most of us here would call ourselves Christian scholars. And, as Reformed Christians, for most of us that means we must do our scholarly work well, in the faith that truth wherever it is found is sacred and revelatory, and therefore should not be, because it cannot be, conformed to a truth different from and higher than itself. To learn sacred things one must discover what one does not expect to discover. If we are loyal to the belief that the great and mysterious truth of God irradiates, permeates existence, like the primal energy that is the origin and substance of all temporal reality, then we have every motive any scholar or poet or philosopher or mystic could want to work freely and deeply, with all the integrity we can muster. Here the word "work" arises again, changed by the fact that it has an object. If in place of "work" I were to say enacted faith, or love, or wonder, that would be closer to my meaning. Calvin's beautiful teaching that the only true knowledge of God is born of obedience means, among other things, that knowledge is the fruit of enactment. In seeing obedience to God as a means by which the grace of God is to be made present to those around us, he urges an open and imaginative attentiveness – a gracious attentiveness – to all our companions, all humankind, that is, to God himself in the form in which he has made himself critically accessible to our reverence and to our contempt. No aspect of life is anything other than a radical question, and, if we had the mind for it, a yet more radical discovery.

No doubt I seem to be about to launch an attack on dogmatism, and indeed I am, though not in the ordinary sense of that word. The dogmatism I wish to challenge is not religious but scholarly or academic. It is deeply characteristic of Christian scholarship, however – if not the very creature of it, then certainly its foster child. I am speaking of the so-called "higher criticism," historical criticism, the documentary hypothesis. If I seem obscurantist in taking exception to it, if I, a mere literary type, seem to be taking on the great minds and the revered figures in a complex field in which I have doubtful competence, then it must be said that anyone who ever challenged dogma has been thought of in the same terms. When a dogma is well established, competence is taken to mean deference to it. Dogma is teaching; therefore it is what the learned ought to have learned.

I am indeed a scholar and teacher of literature, a writer and a teacher of writers. And, need I say, the Bible is a literature. Much of English language literature after the Reformation is an exploration of forms learned from the

Bible. The scenic structure of Shakespeare's plays is modeled closely on the kind of narrative structure one finds in Genesis. I would say something so straightforward as that a literary interpretation of the Bible should be authoritative if not decisive in establishing the fundamental integrity of Scripture – specifically of the Old Testament – were it not true that there is a school of interpretation long current in the study of literature as a whole which is indebted to Biblical scholarship for terminology (notably *exegesis* and *hermeneutics)*, for offish and scholastic impenetrability, for perfect confidence that any apparent meaning of the text is at best very obliquely related to its actual meaning, and that the writer is a sort of primitive whose true intentions are obscure to herself but accessible to those schooled in "theory." We children of the Reformation should be aware that this is all quite medieval in its impulses and in its consequences. As an approach to Scripture and to secular literature it is *dis*integrative. It defeats narrative in its function as carrier of meaning. The signature of dogmatism is that it insists on its own priority over the very texts on whose significance its claims to authority are based. The notion is that these texts can only be correctly interpreted when they confirm the dogmatic/critical assumptions brought to them, and they are defective or negligible to the extent that they fail to be conformable to such interpretation. This is simply not the way good scholarship is done.

We do not know and we will never know how the Bible was written and collected. How an ancient culture would have dealt with the development and preservation of a literature it considered sacred is a question nothing in our experience qualifies us to address with any confidence at all. For a long time it has been considered naive to read the Bible as a coherent document whose content and form reflect the good faith and the theological wisdom of those responsible for its creation and transmission. Somehow the fact that we do not know and cannot know how the Bible came to be has transformed itself into the certainty that we know more or less exactly how it came to be, and that it is grossly unsophisticated to think otherwise. Declining belief in a historical Jesus is compensated, if that is the word, by unquestioning belief in a historical Jahwist. The little mists of hypothesis that surround this figure – sometimes there are several of him, he has appeared to Harold Bloom in the form of a woman – simply authenticate him as the product of scholarship, which he certainly is. The question that must be asked is whether the scholarship that conjured him is sound and reasonable.

"Higher criticism" is about two hundred years old now, and full of that dreadful old certainty that made its sibling enthusiasms – anthropology, racial science, eugenics, philology, and so on – so overwhelming in their influence on modern thought. It is astonishing how naive it all was in what it thought it knew. Of course, "Jahweh" would be revealed to these savants as an autochthonous warrior god. It was just such a god they were looking for. The discovery confirmed fashionable insights into the origins of religion and culture. And it flew in the face of Enlightenment universalism, which has been unfashionable in important circles for as long as it has had a name. The Reformation gave great prominence to the Old Testament, and the rise of anti-Semitism during this period made its demotion to a primitive tribal epic, derivative and patched and in general much inferior to the Greeks, a labor of scholarship congenial to many and of help in the propagation of anti-Semitism. The notion that religion is essentially tribal and national encouraged Aryan paganism on one hand and the ghastly accommodation called German Christianity on the other.

There are flaws and glitches in the Biblical texts, of course. Allowances for human fallibility must always be made. But they must be made consistently and advisedly, not reserved for the scrutiny of ancient texts. If there is any body of thought to be approached with the deepest suspicion and the gravest alertness to political and factional distortion or contamination, it is surely the scholarship of early modern Europe, which found its disordered and cynical image so compellingly present in the Old and the New Testaments. Yet here we are after much time and disaster, cherishing their dubious old insights as if they were objectivity itself.

When I speak of Christian scholarship I do not use the word "Christian" casually. I do not intend to indicate by it an academic specialization, or an ethnicity, or an accustomed loyalty, or a moral or an aesthetic sympathy, though a great deal that has been said and done and written in the name of Christianity comes from these quarters. I mean the scholarship of the faithful, who are no doubt as numerous now, and as touching and impressive to those with an eye for such things, as they were in the church before the Reformation. It is entirely possible to do bad work in good faith, especially when the impulse to venerate one's predecessors, which is a strong component of the religious temperament, makes one's own work a credulous appropriation of earlier bad work. From my own reading, especially in Old Testament studies, I take uncritical deference and its consequences to be somewhere between common and typical. I regret that I am forced to generalize from what is indeed a slight acquaintance with this literature, but I cannot really apologize, because the gist is so easily gotten, and the methodology is so consistent in its assumptions and so unreflectingly relentless in its alienation from the text, that I can promise you I will never know it much better than I do now.

But I will look for a moment at a highly reputable instance of the kind of scholarship I have in mind, Walter Brueggemann's *Theology of the Old Testament*. By his own account, Brueggemann is not so innocent, not so naive, as to accept the claims of any era in the development of Scriptural interpretation to being transparent, free of the inevitable biases of its particular historical moment. This is surely commendable, in principle. In fact, however, in his Introduction to *Theology of the Old Testament* he misrepresents Western intellectual history in general, and grossly misrepresents the crucial period in which documentary criticism arose. With the best will in the world, it is hard to be sensitive to the biases of a period with which one is not familiar. To quote only one example, Brueggemann says:

> The period 1814-1914, which featured the high period of historical criticism in Scripture study, was a time of great intellectual ferment in Europe, and of enormous cultural development, along with a political climate that permitted confidence in reason and buoyancy about human autonomy and progress. It fostered the belief that everything human was now possible. While there is not a one-to-one correspondence between this general mood and the Wellhausen consensus, it is plausible that the hypothesis could have arisen only in the context of a widely shared sense of well-being and self-congratulation.

> As the development of the scholarly consensus of progressivism in revelation reflected a cultural setting of well-being, so the challenges to the hypothesis that arose in the twentieth century also reflected a specific cultural context. The Great War of 1914-18 with its disastrous culmination in the Treaty of Versailles witnessed powerfully against any naive optimism and against any confidence in the human capacity to construct an adequate world, to say nothing of an adequate hypothesis of progressive developmentalism. The Western situation after 1918 required a fresh recognition of the tenuousness of the human situation and the power of evil in the world.[3]

So, in his view, 1814-1914 was a period of heady optimism. By his lights, nothing intervened to dash Europe's sense of well-being. I would suggest, however, that if 1830 does not seem notable to Walter Brueggemann, it did to Charles Baudelaire, and if 1848 does not seem significant to Walter Brueggemann, it did to Karl Marx, and if 1870-71 is not striking to Walter Brueggemann, it was to Friedrich Nietzsche, and to Otto von Bismarck, and to the younger Helmuth von Moltke, and to any number of European nationalists and militarists. In each of these years European governments fought major battles within and against their own cities. In the last of them, Paris, the cultural capital of Europe, was besieged, shelled, and starved into submission with terrible loss of life by the government at Versailles. As Tolstoy documents in *The Kingdom of God Is within You,* many distinguished thinkers of the period were indeed optimistic *about the imminence of a great European war,* which would in their view be culturally tonic and socially hygienic.[4] Optimism of the kind Brueggemann seems to have in mind is not to be found, however.

I go on at such length because Brueggemann, in this same introduction, likens the claims of Scriptural scholarship and criticism, as it has developed and amassed over the centuries since the Reformation, to the Magisterium of the Roman Catholic Church as articulated by the Council of Trent. The tradition of interpretation of the text must be accepted as having authority in its own right, in his view. Now, putting aside any number of lesser objections, I wish to make the point here that if this same Scriptural scholarship, of which Brueggemann is a well respected practitioner, cannot demonstrate a reasonable grasp of the relatively proximate 19th century in familiar and well-documented Europe, then there is absolutely no reason to accept its constructions of the politics and power relations of ancient Israel. The Reformers did not reject the interpretive authority of the Church because of any quarrel with the theory behind it, which is very attractive. They rejected it because, in fact, they found disparity to the point of radical contradiction between the interpretation and the text. Just so, it would be a splendid thing to feel confident that the accretion of scholarship and criticism over the last few centuries has been in fact, and not only in theory, an accretion of knowledge and insight. But there are disparities far too glaring to be ignored. And whatever may be said for the virtues of ecclesiastical piety, there are no grounds at all for the kind of academic piety that is manifest when these disparities *are* ignored. As I said earlier, Reformed piety is the best possible scholarship. We cannot owe the tradition, or God Himself, anything other or anything less.

I have made the experiment here of transgressing the bounds of decorum. I have been harsh – not for the first time in my life, granted. Is it Christian to say that Christian scholars, in a great many instances past and present, do not hold themselves to appropriate scholarly standards? It must be said in any case. The Reformation reflected the conviction on the part of Luther and Calvin and others that poor teaching had been grossly damaging to the faith in their time. Their famous *sola Scriptura* was not a call to bibliolatry, as is often suggested. It was a call to humanist rigor, to scrupulous and deeply informed attentiveness to a text whose complexities they, as linguists, encountered continuously. As great writers, they knew also that they were encountering a singularly beautiful literature. And, after all, a literature is a more or less explicit modulation of aesthetic effect, just like music. Calvin particularly developed his theology around his interpretation of the Old Testament as a body of great narrative, rejecting the practice common to pre-Reformation and to modern interpreters, of seeing it as so many crepuscular survivals of a primitive cultus. Supersessionism, that bad old impulse, at least acknowledged a passage here and there, in the prophets usually, with a beauty that made it, to their mind, an anticipation of the coming of Christ. Now the New Testament, through the work of John Dominic Crossan, John Shelby Spong, and others, is itself so diminished in general esteem that the concept "supersession" has become meaningless. The refusal to acknowledge the appropriateness of respectful aesthetic attentiveness to any art is what we call

Philistinism or barbarism. These terms do not signify bad form simply. They signify incomprehension.

Luther and Calvin felt that poor teaching had done harm to Christianity. And how is the faith faring among us now? It abides strongly in the form sometimes called pietism, even among the least conservative Christians, those who are perhaps most exposed to the disintegrative approach to Scripture, and who are therefore most insecure if not impoverished in their vocabulary of faith, that is, in their confidence in the integrity and meaningfulness of the narratives that stand at the center of Christianity and particularly of Protestantism. In many cases they seem to cling to a core belief that would sound naive to them if they were to articulate it. These are my co-religionists, who, I believe, are right in rejecting many fundamentalist tenets for which indubitable Scriptural authority is claimed, and wrong to believe that Scripture does indeed endorse them. Perhaps some part of their and their pastors' receptivity to "higher criticism" arises from the thought that the biblical authority claimed by fundamentalism can be, and even ought to be, diminished by a partial or conditional rejection of the authority of the Bible itself. This is a very costly concession to make and terrible loss to suffer. But the primitivity discovered in the text by academic criticism reinforces the assumption on every side that the teaching of Scripture, especially the Old Testament, is likely to be very simple and also, depending on cases, very harsh.

This new medievalism is overwhelmingly a Protestant contribution to our present befuddlements, though the Catholics are gaining on us rapidly. History the ironist must take especial pleasure in *our* having made the Bible a veiled and doubtful text intelligible only to specialists. I have heard that many pastors preach the text as their congregations expect to hear it preached, knowing as they do so that it is taught far differently in the seminaries. In other words, they do not preach in good faith, they do not believe what they say. What a terrible breach of candor and respect to exist at the heart of a church. It is a new esotericism, with the great and painful difference that the hidden doctrine is not sacred or even interesting. To use a metaphor from the Reformation, it claims to be a knowledge of the devices and mechanisms by which the figures of sacred narrative have been made to *seem* to move and weep and bleed. Then there are those who make, by their lights, a liberal and enlightened theology by combining this hermeneutics of suspicion with virtuous sentiments and the doing of good. However conscientious, this is, I believe, an even more regrettable choice, since it instills the same cynicism in the congregation and effectively desensitizes them to the text. This posture considers itself to be at the furthest extreme from dogmatism, yet it is dogmatism in that it imposes what it knows in contempt of what it might discover.

Imposition of this kind is always the destroyer of narrative, which depends on the granting of integrity in order to contain its complex and particular meaning. If musicologists were to go over the canon of Western music and excise those portions which violated convention, which were not consistent with the development of the art of composition at the time they were said to have been written, which sound like another composer than the one to which they are attributed, or which, in these specialists' judgment, would be more appropriate elsewhere in the piece or in another piece altogether, at the end of it all we would have something much less than the canon of Western music. So with the disruption of narrative, which, like music, develops its meaning over the time it claims for that development. Any good art makes choices that startle and even aggrieve critics and scholars. Such choices are rarely distinguishable from whatever anomalies might arise from faulty transmission or from scribal emendations. And neither can they be distinguished with confidence from anomalies, which are nothing more than artifacts of misspent scholarly diligence. On grounds of antiquity alone, whatever an intact biblical narrative might contain is of vastly greater interest than the case any scholar can make for dismembering it.

As I have said, I am teaching a seminar on the Old Testament to students at the Writers' Workshop. It is a large class and well attended, the latter fact significant because students have no papers or exams or presentations in these classes, and they receive no grades. We offer seminars we hope they will find valuable, with the understanding that nothing should take time away from their writing unless they do indeed find it valuable. I teach the same class concurrently at my church. Many of my Workshop students have told me that they know nothing at all about the Bible because they have no religious background, or despite casual Catholic or Protestant instruction in childhood, or even despite a devout parent or family or a parochial education. The people who take the class at my church typically have some familiarity with the Old Testament, yet those with a substantial knowledge of it, even those with divinity school behind them, have no very meaningful sense of it. Knowing Genesis and not knowing it at all are effectively equivalent because those who study it learn that it is fundamentally incoherent. The perceived absence of integral narrative yields a perceived absence of meaning.

Discussing the Joseph narrative in Genesis, my class arrived at the conclusion that the justice of God is not equity – it is mercy. How could such a complex understanding be arrived at except by means of an intensely artful narrative? What vision of grace do any of us have that does not rise out of narrative? To have disrupted the perceived coherence of the Scriptures, which are the birthright of every Christian and would-be Christian in this sad and pious country, is a grave thing indeed. If I am any judge, it has been done on the basis of scholarly pretexts, which are slender at very best. I feel strongly that the most urgent work of Christian scholarship is to acknowledge and redress the damage done by Christian scholarship.

---

[1] Walter Brueggemann, *Theology of the Old Testament: Testimony, Dispute, Advocacy* (Minneapolis: Fortress Press, 1997), 673.

[2] "We can be moral without religion: The end of Christianity is no bad thing," *The Observer* (London), 9 September 2001, Leaders.

[3] Brueggemann, 15.

[4] Leo Tolstoy, *The kingdom of God is within you: Christianity not as a mystic religion but as a new theory of life,* trans. Constance Garnett (1894; reprint, Lincoln: University of Nebraska Press, 1984).

Christian Scholarship and Human Responsibility

John Hare

The title of this lecture, "Christian Scholarship and Human Responsibility," is not very revealing. I am going to talk about something narrower in scope, though still adventurous. I want to look at the question of whether we can find an evolutionary basis for human morality.

There is a whole field of evolutionary ethics that would answer this question, "Yes." Some version is likely to become the mainstream view in the academic study of ethics over the next few years. I am not a scientist, but a philosopher. So I am not going to try to pass judgment on the theory of evolution itself, as it applies to human beings. I do not regard philosophers as professionally competent either to pass a positive or negative judgment on the theory, except insofar as there are philosophical commitments embodied in it. However, I do regard myself as having made some progress in understanding human morality. In particular, I have been interested in and have written about the gap between the demands of morality on us and our natural capacities to meet those demands. This gap presents the problem of how we can be held accountable or responsible for a standard we are not equipped to meet either by innate capacity or natural development. So I want to ask the conditional question: *if* we assume that the theory of evolution as it applies to human beings is correct, does this help us answer the questions of whether we *can* be morally good and why we *should* be morally good? The first question, whether we *can* be morally good, is the question raised by the moral gap between the demands of morality and our natural capacities. It is only after answering this first question, "yes, we can be morally good," that the second question arises of why we *should* be morally good, for we can only be held accountable or responsible for standards that we are able to reach. The burden of my presentation will be that we do *not* get an answer to these two questions from the theory of evolution. I am not arguing here that the theory is false, but that *even if* it is true, it doesn't give us an answer. I will be looking at a number of recent attempts to provide such an answer from the theory, but I will claim that all of them fail.

The Nature of Human Morality

In order to answer my conditional question, I need to lay out first what I take the nature of human morality to be. There are many different philosophical accounts here to choose from. I am going to give you mine, without trying to prove its superiority to its major rivals. That would be a different project. The account I am going to give takes its inspiration from John Duns Scotus, a Franciscan theologian and philosopher of the late Middle Ages. He formulated what he had already found in Anselm of Canterbury and, before Anselm, in Augustine. It may seem odd to bring a fourteenth-century theologian and philosopher into contact in this way with twenty-first century evolutionary theory, but in order to understand an idea philosophically, one has to look at its genealogy and its material embodiments in culture. Ideas arise in a conversation across the generations, and we cannot see any particular idea clearly until we see the conversational context in which it emerges.

Take the idea of right and wrong. Duns Scotus had the idea that what makes something right is that God commands it, and that we have access to this righteousness or justice by a special affection of the will, which Scotus calls "the affection for justice." This is a technical phrase, and I am not going to use technical philosophical terms in this lecture except for this one and its contrast phrase, "the affection for advantage." An affection, in Scotus' sense, is an inclination or movement in the will towards something. And justice is, in the classical conception, not a narrowly defined idea of distributing to people what they have a right to, but righteousness in general, or moral goodness itself. The Good Samaritan in Jesus' parable (Luke 10:30-37) showed the affection for justice in being moved by the plight of the man wounded by the side of the road, even though that man was a traditional enemy of his race. The affection for justice is drawn towards the good in itself and thus to God, without reference to any advantage to the self. Loving an enemy is the paradigm case because it so clearly leaves behind the self and its extensions to others in one's community and tribe. On the other hand, the affection for advantage is an inclination or movement in the will towards one's own happiness.

There is nothing wrong with wanting to be happy, or with being concerned about oneself, but what counts morally is the ranking of the two affections. Take, for example, my giving this lecture. I might have two different kinds of motives as I lecture. I might be giving my attention to the subject matter for its own sake, and to you, my audience, trying to communicate to you as well as I know how. Or I might be psychologically focused on myself delivering the lecture and trying to make you like or admire *me*. This example illustrates that our motivational and affective state is usually a mixture, and this is what Duns Scotus says. I have both affections as I lecture here, both the affection for advantage and the affection for justice, and they operate in me simultaneously. The key moral question, however, is how I *rank* the two. There is nothing wrong with a concern for my own happiness. Scotus says that we were created with it, and we will have it even in heaven. God wants our happiness, even more than we want it. After telling us to love our enemies, Jesus goes on to talk about reward. But if the affection for advantage is ranked first, it will become an *improper* regard for the self. The proper ranking is that we are to seek *first* the kingdom of God and his righteousness, and then the other things will be added to us. An extreme form of this thought is the expression Jonathan Edwards uses in *Religious Affections* (part III, chapter X), "to be even willing to be damned for the glory of God." Edwards is echoing the words of Moses and also of Paul (Romans 9:3; Exodus 32:32; see also Matthew 27:45). He is not saying that God in fact requires such a sacrifice, but that he would choose this ranking if God did require it. Our problem after the Fall is not, Scotus says, that we are born with the affection for advantage, but that we are born with a wrongful ranking of the two affections. And we are not able, by ourselves, to reverse this ranking, since the preference for the self already underlies all our choices. Changing this ranking requires God's assistance.

Duns Scotus was the most influential philosopher in Europe for about two hundred years after his death; both Luther and Calvin learned their philosophy in this context. I do not want to exaggerate here. As far as we know, Calvin and Luther did not read Scotus himself, but they were both educated in institutions where Scotus was taught. And the basic framework of Scotus can be seen in their work – in particular in their versions of the divine command theory of ethics and in their distrust of self-love. Thus Calvin says, "God's will is so much the highest rule of righteousness that whatever he wills, by the very fact that he wills it, must be considered righteous"; and he locates in our self-love the principal obstacle to our obedience to God's will.[1]

From Luther, the German pietists learned the same theory, and we find the same basic framework in the most important philosopher of modern times, Immanuel Kant, who himself grew up in a pietist Lutheran home. Kant says that we should recognize our duties as God's commands, and that our respect for this duty has the power to overcome the love of the dear self.[2] The great twentieth-century ethicists in both Continental and Anglo-American philosophy have defined themselves in terms of supporting or opposing Kant. But they have mostly tried to do this without the theistic framework that Kant felt he had to appeal to in order to make sense of morality. By unmooring or untying morality from theism, they have given their systems a highly characteristic kind of nervousness or hesitancy. This is what Nietzsche foretold at the end of the nineteenth century as a period of "convalescence" after, what he called, the death of God.

I do not want to go further into the details of this history. I hope I have said enough to make it plausible that the ideas we now have about right and wrong both have a long lineage or pedigree, and cannot be understood without going back into this history.

Going back to Scotus, then, we can see how he connects morality and freedom, and the same basic connection can be found in Kant. Freedom is implied in the ability to rank the two affections of justice and advantage. Scotus says that we only have freedom because we have both of them, the affection for justice in addition to the affection for advantage. If we had merely the affection for advantage, like non-human animals, we would not be free, because we would pursue our own advantage by necessity. Here Scotus departs from another tradition in Western philosophy, which we can find in its purest form amongst the ancient Greeks, in Plato and Aristotle, for example. The understanding of happiness in Greek philosophy is complex, but for both these thinkers, every motivation that we have is in the end to be understood as a motivation towards our own happiness. Scotus expresses a different thought, though it is not original with Scotus. As I said earlier, he found it in Anselm of Canterbury, and there is a strain of it in Augustine (where Anselm learned it). It is Augustine who first introduces the idea of this kind of will into philosophy, but he is articulating what he finds in the scriptures as repentance, the idea of a fundamental reorientation of the heart away from the old man and towards the kingdom of God. Augustine is here, I believe, being faithful to the New Testament and to the Hebrew scriptures. But Scotus' thought, though not original, *is* different from the Greeks. Unlike Plato and Aristotle, Scotus sees that we have within us the possibility of choosing to rank something else above our own happiness. What gives us this possibility is hearing the call of God, whose goodness so far transcends us that it has the power to reduce our self-love, our affection for advantage, to submission. It is this call, therefore, and our ability to hear it, which lies behind our freedom. In the Greeks, there is no freedom in this sense, and there is no will in the sense that a part of us does this fundamental ranking. The title of my presentation, "Christian Scholarship and Human Responsibility," takes off from this thought of Scotus, for it is only beings who are free who have responsibility. There can be causal responsibility without freedom, as when we say an enormous meteor is responsible for wiping out the dinosaurs, but without freedom there cannot be moral responsibility or accountability.

The Problem of the Gaps

If this picture of human morality is right, it leaves us with two kinds of gaps. First, there is what I will call the "affection gap" between those animals who have only the affection for advantage and humans who have also the affection for justice. Second, there is the "performance gap" within our own lives between the demand to be moral and our actual performance. Being moral demands a revolution of the will. Before the revolution we have a set of priorities: we will only do what we see to be good if we can see that it will make us happy. But morality demands a kind of revolution or reversal of those priorities: that we do only what we think will make us happy if we can see that it is in itself good. In other words, the moral demand is to rank the affection for justice over the affection for advantage. A consequence of this is that we are not allowed morally to give ourselves any greater moral weight or importance than we give any other human being. For my goodness or worth is not in itself any greater than anyone else's. We *do* have, as human beings ourselves, the same moral weight as any other, so that we are also not allowed morally to make ourselves doormats for other people to walk on. We also have a greater responsibility for ourselves than we do for others, because we control our own lives more directly. But morally we all count the same.

Now, if this is the moral demand, there is a performance gap between it and the natural capacities with which we are born. We are born, Scotus and Kant agree, with the wrongful ranking of the two affections, and we cannot without assistance change this. So, it looks as though there is a kind of incoherence in the moral life, the incoherence of holding ourselves to a standard that we are unable to reach. Christianity, however, gives us an additional element in this picture. God is seen as the source of the moral demand on us. Moreover, as Augustine says, "God commands some things which we cannot do, in order that we may know what we ought to ask of Him. For this is faith itself, which obtains by prayer what the law commands."[3] Upon first hearing this sounds odd, as though God is holding us accountable to a standard we are unable to reach. But Augustine is not saying we cannot reach the standard; he is saying we cannot reach it on our own, or by our own devices. Luther uses the illustration of a parent who tells his young child to walk to him. The child takes a few steps and totters, and then reaches out for the help of the parent's hand, which is offered to bring him the rest of the way.[4] Moreover, God intervenes in our lives to change us so that we can live by the demand. God does this by revealing something of the divine nature to us, as Paul says in Romans, and this revelation has the power to subordinate our love of the self and our affection for advantage, and so to change the ranking of the two affections in us (Romans 1:20). Then the apparent incoherence I mentioned of holding us to an impossible standard disappears.

Before leaving this account of human morality, I want to point to one curious feature of contemporary moral philosophy in the Kantian tradition. In much of this philosophy we still find the idea of an imaginary being who is the source of the moral demand and whose prescriptions are authoritative for us. This notion has survived even amongst theorists (and this is the large majority) who no longer believe in God. They call this imaginary being various names, such as "the impartial spectator" or "the archangel," and they insist that talking in this way is merely a heuristic device, useful for conceptual clarity.[5] They do not suppose that there is in fact such a being, or that such a being gives us the kind of assistance that the Christian tradition proclaims. These theorists are therefore left with the kind of incoherence I have been talking about, namely the incoherence of holding us accountable to a standard we are unable to meet. This is one source of the nervousness or hesitancy I mentioned earlier.

Contemporary moral philosophy uses at least three strategies to get over the problem of the performance gap without invoking God's assistance. I mention these three strategies here because we will see examples of all three of them in the literature on evolutionary ethics. The first strategy is to hold our natural capacities where they are on the traditional picture and reduce the moral demand in order to fit them. The second strategy is to keep the moral demand where it is on the traditional picture and exaggerate or puff up our natural capacity to meet this demand. The third strategy is to hold both the demand and our capacities constant, and then find some naturalistic substitute to do God's work in bridging the resultant gap. This picture of the moral gap is a very familiar picture of how we tend to think about morality in the Western world; it is familiar even amongst those who no longer believe in God. But there are problems internal to this picture about *how* we can live morally and *why* we should live morally; and the theory of evolution cannot significantly help us with these problems.

The Affection Gap

Having given briefly an account of what human morality is like, we can now return to sociobiology and evolutionary ethics. I want to deal separately with the two gaps I talked about. First, the affection gap. Nowhere in the literature about non-human animals have I found an example of what Scotus calls the affection for justice, but only complicated forms of the affection for advantage. Scotus himself suggested there was this kind of difference between us and non-human animals: they do not have the affection for justice. This means that they do not have freedom of the Scotist kind either, since, if Scotus is right, it is only beings who have the affection for justice that have this kind of freedom. In the next part of this lecture I will discuss what I called the performance gap. I will claim that evolutionary ethics does not resolve the problem of the gap between our aspirations to meet the moral demand and our actual performance, the gap (to put it colloquially) between our talk and our walk.

In dealing with these two gaps separately, I am responding to two different arguments that can be found in evolutionary ethics. The first argument is that we can understand how humans can be morally good by looking at the source of this goodness in capacities that non-human animals already have. This makes human goodness non-mysterious and forestalls the need to appeal to anything spooky, like the assistance of God. By claiming that there is an affection gap, I am saying that there is something crucial about human morality that is not found in non-human animals. Evolutionary ethics also makes a second argument, which concerns the performance gap. Even if they cannot appeal to common origin to explain human moral capacity, they can appeal to evolutionary pressure during early periods of human history. On this view, human morality is just like every other part of human life, or the life of any species for that matter: the fundamental explanation is in terms of natural selection or adaptation, and hence reproductive advantage. I am going to claim that there is something crucial about human morality that cannot be explained by locating its source in natural selection.

Let us consider the affection gap, then. What do I mean by saying that non-human animals have only complicated forms of the affection for advantage, and do not have the affection for justice? I will give three examples: from the social insects, from vampire bats, and from chimpanzees. The first example is of kin selection, the second of so-called reciprocal altruism, and the third of social control. These are all forms of self-benefit. Darwin says, in one of his moods, "Natural selection will never produce in a being anything injurious to itself, for natural selection acts solely by and for the good of each."[6] But according to Scotus, the affection for justice leads to a radical willingness to sacrifice the self. I already quoted the phrase from Jonathan Edwards about being willing to be damned for the glory of God.

The social insects have been a model of morality from the time of Homer and Virgil. Isaac Watts exclaims,

> How doth the little busy bee
>> Improve each shining hour,
> And gather honey all the day,
>> From ev'ry opening flow'r![7]

For a Darwinist, what is especially confounding is the abstinence from sexual reproduction of whole groups of bees and ants. Darwin himself declared that the insects posed a "special difficulty, which at first appeared to me insuperable, and actually fatal to my whole theory."[8] The problem is that the most basic feature of his theory is that those variations within a species that leave more offspring will tend to be preserved and gradually become the norm. How could a variation that produced celibacy be successful from an evolutionary point of view? While he speculated that the abstinence might be explained by some kind of group selection, he was never satisfied that he had found the solution.

A solution has been found, however, and its discovery is what gave the impetus to the first great wave of sociobiology in the early 1970's, culminating in the publication of E. O. Wilson's *Sociobiology* in 1975.[9] In 1977 I went to a six-week conference called "Biological and Sociological Perspectives on Human Nature," and the furious reaction to Wilson was in full swing, with the main speakers being Stephen Jay Gould and Dick Levin, an ant specialist from Harvard. I remember a whole afternoon on hands and knees in the Garden of the Gods in Colorado in the middle of July looking at ant battles in the sand.

The solution to the problem of the sterile casts among social insects was kin selection. It turns out that many of the social insects (ants, wasps, and bees) have a reproductive structure, which results in the workers being more closely related genetically to their sisters from the same queen than to any offspring they might have themselves. We can think of the sterility of the workers, therefore, as promoting a greater dispersion of their genes in the next generation by working for the survival of the rest of the colony than by their own reproduction. Here is a solution to the problem of apparent altruism amongst the social insects, which brings it in line with the survival of the fittest. But note that we have nothing here that takes us beyond the affection for advantage into the affection for justice. Compare kin selection with the parable of the Good Samaritan, who was not related by blood or tribe and was, in fact, a traditional enemy of the man who was wounded by the side of the road, whom he loaded onto his donkey and whose expenses at the inn he paid himself. The affection for justice requires my action on behalf of someone without regard to that person's relation to myself, merely because I see he or she is in need.

My second example is so-called "reciprocal altruism" amongst vampire bats who live on blood. They go out at night on hunting expeditions; sometimes they are successful and sometimes not. After two or three days without blood, they starve. But to deal with this problem, they have evolved a buddy system according to which the successful hunters will regurgitate some of the blood into the mouths of their unsuccessful buddies.[10] It is not altogether clear whether this kind of reciprocity can be detached from kin selection because the association into bat-clusters may be a marker for kinship. In any case, suppose here we do have something like reciprocity between unrelated members of the same species.

We can now model these interactions using game theory, which works out which strategies between two or more players of a game might be stable, if repeated a very large number of times. In the present context, stability means that the strategy could be fitness maximizing, and it turns out that co-operation can be a fitness-maximizing strategy under certain conditions. For example, one such strategy that has been modeled is what is called "tit-for-tat," where benefits and harms are both reciprocated. It turns out that this is only stable, however, if there is massive reliability in the reception of signals from the other players. In the real world, where there are so many incentives to disguise real intentions, this kind of reliability is unlikely. Maybe there are other strategies that can be shown to work. It is not my concern to argue this one way or the other. My point is just that we are still within the range of the affection for advantage. One way to illustrate this is to compare tit-for-tat with the reply Socrates first gets in the *Republic,* when he asks what justice is. The reply is: Justice is to do good to your friends and harm to your enemies,[11] and most Greeks of Socrates' time would have said the same thing. I suspect that common sense still holds much the same opinion. For Socrates, by contrast, it is always wrong to do harm, even in retaliation against your enemies.[12] In the same way, Jesus says in the Sermon on the Mount, "You have heard that it was said, 'You shall love your neighbor and hate your enemy.' But I say to you, Love your enemies and pray for those who persecute you" (Matthew 5:43-44 Revised Standard Version).

My third example is about social control amongst chimpanzees, from an anecdote told by Frans de Waal in his delightful book *Good Natured.*

Jimoh, the current alpha male of the Yerkes Field Station group, once detected a secret mating between Socko, an adolescent male, and one of Jimoh's favorite females. Socko and the female had wisely disappeared from view, but Jimoh had gone looking for them. Normally, the old male would merely chase off the culprit, but for some reason – perhaps because the female had repeatedly refused to mate with Jimoh himself that day – he this time went full speed after Socko and did not give up. He chased him all around the enclosure – Socko screaming and defecating in fear, Jimoh intent on catching him.

Before he could accomplish his aim, several females close to the scene began to "woaow" bark. This indignant sound is used in protest against aggressors and intruders. At first the callers looked around to see how the rest of the group was reacting; but when others joined in, particularly the top-ranking female, the intensity of their calls quickly increased until literally everyone's voice was part of a deafening chorus. The scattered beginning almost gave the impression that the group was taking a vote. Once the protest had swelled to a chorus, Jimoh broke off his attack with a nervous grin on his face: he got the message. Had he failed to respond, there would no doubt have been concerted female action to end the disturbance.[13]

Now, some caution is necessary here. Frans de Waal is famous for imputing human-like intentions to apes. In this narrative, he uses terms like "indignant," "taking a vote," "nervous grin," "got the message." All of this is tendentious, in the sense (as he admits) that it begs the very questions about intentionality that he is trying to answer. But suppose we grant him the description. What the anecdote gives us is an example of chimpanzees following something like a prescriptive rule for challenging behavior (in this case by the alpha male) that seriously endangers the cohesion of the group. There is something almost moral here, what de Waal calls a "precursor" to morality. In terms of the distinction from Scotus, there is not yet the affection for justice. This protest by the female chimps is indeed directed at the welfare of a vulnerable member of their group, but it is still their group. What seems to be going on here is a form of social control in which rules that are beneficial to the group are enforced by a kind of communal sanction.

So we do not get, in any of these three cases, any example that requires us to bring in the affection for justice. We do not know, to be sure, that there is no affection for justice, since we could not see into these animals' hearts, even if they did have hearts in the relevant sense. Perhaps the bees or the vampire bats or the chimps do have the same two affections we do, and merely have a performance gap just like us. But in the absence of compelling evidence, it seems better to stick with the language of "precursors" of morality. I think what we get here are various complex forms of the affection for advantage. But still, the analysis of kin selection and reciprocal altruism and social control are interesting for the moral philosopher. According to the moral theory I started with, we are born with a mixture of two affections. By describing in other species one part of this mixture, the affection for advantage, these analyses give us fresh detail about the moral gap. The kind of evolutionary psychology I have been describing could give us an understanding of just how close the affection gap comes to being bridged naturally, and yet what differences between humans and non-human animals still remain.

The Performance Gap

In the rest of this lecture I will reply to three kinds of attempts in the recent literature on evolutionary ethics to provide an answer to the problem of the *performance* gap, the gap between our talk and our walk. These are attempts to bridge the gap without bringing in God's assistance. This section of the talk will be the hardest to follow because I will be referring to several different authors and the details of their arguments. In order to organize these references, I will use the framework of the three strategies I mentioned earlier for dealing with the problem of the moral gap, namely the strategies of reducing the moral demand, puffing up the human capacity, and finding a substitute for God's assistance. These three strategies are used in the contemporary world outside evolutionary ethics, but for the purposes of this talk I want to focus on the examples inside evolutionary ethics, and especially examples of the first strategy. I will mention the other two very briefly at the end.

The First Strategy

The first of these strategies starts by conceding that we naturally rank the self first and motivate all action by our own happiness; and then the strategy re-conceptualizes our situation by reducing the moral demand to fit our natural capacities so described. In that way, there is no longer any moral gap. I am going to discuss two ways of carrying out this strategy, one way in the work of Larry Arnhart, a political theorist, and one way in the work of two very different biologists, Richard Alexander and David Sloan Wilson.

Larry Arnhart starts from two identifications. He says that the good is the desirable, and the desirable is the generally desired.[14] By "generally desired" he means what humans have desired throughout their evolutionary history.[15] This gives especial weight to the great length of the Pleistocene period, when humans were hunter-gatherers and when natural selection presumably exercised most of its effects on variation within human populations. Arnhart accordingly draws up a list of twenty desires that are "generally desired" in this sense. The list includes such items as: high social status, political rule (though this is, he says, a natural male desire not a natural female desire), for war (again a male desire), for wealth (that is, enough property to equip one for a good life and to display social status), and for justice as reciprocity.[16] I will return to this last item in a moment. Many of the items on this list are competitive goods, in the sense that one person can only have them if other people do not. One person can only have high social status if others have lower status, and so on. I want to repeat, though, that for Arnhart the satisfaction of these desires is good, because they are all, in his sense, generally desired.

There is not an affection for justice in Duns Scotus' sense anywhere on the list, though there is a desire for justice as reciprocity. In the language I discussed earlier, there is so-called reciprocal altruism. But Arnhart wants to deny that there is an ethical demand to love our enemies, and he denies that any valid principle of ethics requires impartial benevolence. Neither of these items appears in his evolutionary list of what is generally desired. He recognizes that he is departing here even from Darwin in one of Darwin's moods. For Darwin thought, at least sometimes, that female sympathy – as rooted in maternal care – could expand into a disinterested universal sentiment of humanity.[17] But Arnhart points out that "[a]fter all, even maternal care manifests itself as a love of one's own offspring and a willingness to defend them against strangers. And although sympathy can be expanded to embrace ever-larger groups based on some sense of shared interests, this will always rest on loving one's own group as opposed to other groups. Darwin's appeal to universal humanitarianism can only be explained," Arnhart thinks, "as a utopian yearning for an ideal moral realm that transcends nature, which contradicts Darwin's general claim that human beings are fully contained within the natural order."[18] Arnhart concludes that since humans are *not* "bound together by a universal sentiment of disinterested humanitarianism, then deep conflicts of interest between individuals or between groups can create moral tragedies in which there is no universal moral principle or sentiment to resolve the conflict."[19] He says, "When individuals or groups compete with one another, we must either find some common ground of shared interests, or we must allow for an appeal to force or fraud to settle the dispute. The only alternative, which I do not regard as a realistic alternative, is to invoke some transcendental norm of impartial justice (such as Christian charity) that is beyond the order of nature."[20]

To see the effect of Arnhart's view, consider the case of slavery. Arnhart is not entitled to condemn it morally, since it results from the satisfaction of natural desires for dominance, and he thinks the satisfaction of natural desires is good. The most he is entitled to say is that slavery is tragic, since it results from the conflict of natural desires between the masters and the slaves. Since he thinks there is no universal principle or norm to appeal to, unless there is a common interest, we must allow for an appeal to force or fraud to settle the dispute. Arnhart thinks he can appeal here to reciprocal justice. But reciprocal justice as he defines it requires an expectation of benefit on both sides, or tit-for-tat. Suppose we lived in a society in which those whom we exploited could not harm us because of their relative weakness. Suppose we knew that. We would not be moved by justice as reciprocity to end the exploitation even in the face of our victims' suffering and hatred of us. The restraints of this kind of reciprocal justice would be totally useless. But alas, this has been the situation with slavery for most of its history. The effect of ruling out Scotus' kind of affection for justice as "utopian" is to lower the moral demand to fit our "natural" capacities, or to fit the unconstrained affection for advantage. We will say, for example, that we do not have obligations to starving children in Africa because we do not even know who they are.[21] They are not part of our group. If that is the way our society in fact goes, we will be regressing to tribalism.

The second way to carry out the strategy of reducing the demand does not start out, as does Arnhart, to put normative limits on the moral demand, but it changes the source of the demand, and this has the same effect as reducing its normative force. It locates the origin or source of the moral demand not in God (as Duns Scotus does) but in natural selection or adaptation, and thus in a version of the affection for advantage, either at the level of the genes or at the level of the group. Evolutionary biologists differ in terms of which of these two levels they stress. I will talk about one of each. Twenty-five years after I went to the conference in Colorado, I went to a second conference in 2001 here at Calvin College called "Biology and Purpose: Altruism, Morality, and Human Nature in Evolutionary Theory." I wanted to see if the new form of the theory was liable to the same objections as the old one. Arnhart's book is a good example of the objectionable features of the early sociobiology. But sociobiology has been reborn with the new label "evolutionary psychology," and I wanted to study the similarities and differences between the two movements. Two of the main speakers, both of them biologists, were especially relevant to this project. Richard Alexander was one of the founding figures of sociobiology, especially with his book *Darwinism and Human Affairs*, in 1979.[22] He emphasizes the level of the gene. David Sloan Wilson is one of the new leaders in the field and emphasizes the level of the group. But both biologists locate the source of the affection for justice in the affection for advantage, and I will claim that this ends in reducing or undercutting the moral demand.

Alexander finds in the theory of evolution the fundamental explanation of everything about life, including human life. If there were some part of life that the theory could not explain, the theory would be, he said, a "piddling" theory. The fundamental explanation of all the behaviors of all the various life forms is the final bottom-line pay-off of differential gene replication. Thus religion is to be explained in terms of "one group besting another" and so promoting the survival and reproduction of its members, and moral behavior is to be explained in terms "of enlightened genetic self-interest."[23] Alexander thinks we should base models of the concept of God and of right and wrong on the "reproductive interests of individuals, either as such or as achieved via success of their group," and then we could test those models by measuring differential reproductive rates.[24]

But why should the theory of evolution be seen this way? If we find a part of human life like mathematics that cannot as far as we know be itself explained by evolutionary theory, why should that be construed as a failure in the theory of evolution? This is a telling example because in the early stages of mathematics we find the same kind of hypertrophy of theory. I say "hypertrophy" because it is like the excessive growth of an earlobe or nostril. Pythagoras discovered that some parts of human life, like music, could be explained in terms of ratios of the simple numbers. He went on to urge that "everything is number," and included in the scope of his theory ethics and religion. The logos or harmony of the cosmos is, he said, a triangle, and justice is geometrical equality (or, if I remember this right, the number four). It was this kind of thinking that took over the Academy when Plato died and caused Aristotle to leave it, complaining that we should not confuse ethics and geometry, and that it is the mark of the educated person to seek only that degree of precision that the subject matter allows. Why should we think that because evolution explains some important features of life, it therefore has to explain all of them? Half-humorously, in the spirit of evolutionary ethics, let me suggest that perhaps there is a discrete cognitive module in our brains, which leads us to expand theories globally when they are only locally appropriate.

Alexander's view is that humans invented mathematics, and therefore mathematics has to be understood fundamentally in terms of genetic self-promotion, just like religion or any other feature of life. But then this claim is no longer a part of the theory of evolution, but it is a metaphysical view added onto it: that every domain above the physical and the chemical which human life encounters is to be explained ultimately by natural selection at the genetic level. It is important to see that this metaphysical view cannot itself be justified biologically; it is, I believe, an article of faith for Alexander, though it is not recognized as such. If we deny this metaphysical view, we can say that human life brings us into contact with all sorts of domains, like mathematics or ethics or religion, which are not themselves subject to evolutionary explanation, although evolution may have illuminating things to say about how it is that we have the equipment to access those domains. In saying this, we might still be after a single explanatory theory, but it will be a single theory in a quite different sense. It will be the coherent conjunction of all the different theories that make sense of all our experience, without any expectation that one of these theories has to be the ultimate cash value or bottom line for all the others. Or perhaps "theory" is the wrong word for what we would be after; some less rigorous word like "understanding" is more adequate, since some parts of our experience do not seem to be amenable to theory at all in any rigorous sense.

In contrast to Alexander is David Sloan Wilson, who emphasizes (like Darwin in one of his moods) the role of morality and religion in group selection. Altruistic groups can prosper compared to non-altruistic groups. At the same time selfish individuals within an altruistic group can prosper compared to the altruistic individuals within that same group. This means that the two levels of selection (individual and group) can be in tension, and an adequate explanatory theory has to take account of both. Wilson is more inclined to take seriously the mechanisms of social cohesion within altruistic groups, including their religious and ethical codes, as having themselves selective advantage. He also allows that cultural systems which have adaptive advantage can produce as by-products elements which are themselves adaptively neutral, or even to a limited degree counter-adaptive. But Wilson is no more inclined than Alexander to suppose that the claims internal to the domains of religion and ethics as divine command are *true*. Take, for example, his case study of Calvin's Geneva. Wilson sees Calvin's claims about God's adoption of the elect and the unworthiness of, for example, unduly quarrelsome elders to receive communion as mechanisms of social control, as useful *fictions*. Wilson's analysis is that Geneva was on the verge of dissolution as a viable community before Calvin arrived, and was enabled by Calvinism to prosper in the face of severe external and internal pressure; so its citizens were assisted in their evolutionary role of surviving and reproducing.[25] Although Wilson allows more autonomy to the level of group selection than Alexander, there is still a reduction of the affection for justice to the affection for advantage at the fundamental level of explanation. Adaptation is still, as Wilson says, the gold standard in explanation. Wilson's account is less reductionist than Alexander's, but both biologists have the same metaphysical commitment to a naturalistic explanation for all the phenomena of human life in terms of the theory of evolution.

The Publicity Standard

We can now face both biologists with the problem of what I will call the publicity standard. The publicity standard is that a normative theory should be able to make public what it claims as the source or origin of the normative demand, without thereby undercutting the demand. Here is where we get back to the strategy of reducing the demand. Let me give an example. Suppose we thought that ethical demands and religious authority were both invented by the powerful political elite in order to maintain their power. Some of the sophists suggested this in ancient Greece. The idea was that the powerful wanted to control the weak even in their thoughts, and so they invented the idea of gods who could look at the heart and would punish disobedience and disloyalty. Suppose we discovered that this was the origin of our ethical striving and our religious belief: we had been programmed that way by a culture that was basically under the control of a powerful elite. This discovery would tend to undercut our ethical commitment, which is hard enough to sustain even without such discoveries. If I found that my efforts to be impartially benevolent were programmed into me by BIG BROTHER, I would start to think of myself as Macbeth, a poor player who struts and frets his hour upon the stage, my life full of sound and fury but signifying nothing. Why would these discoveries be undercutting? Because BIG BROTHER is concerned not with right but with his own power.

The discovery that adaptation through group selection was the source or origin of the normative demand would have much the same effect. I would regard myself as programmed by something that was itself at odds with morality. For adaptation is aligned with the affection for advantage. The proposed evolutionary explanation is that it is good for my group in competition with other groups that I feel the demand of the affection for justice. But the affection for justice is required by its nature to be blind to my relationship to one group rather than another, as the Good Samaritan was blind. The proposed explanation therefore undercuts the demand, and therefore fails the publicity standard.

This point is valid also against the views of Michael Ruse, a philosopher who is conspicuous in this field. Ruse holds that the objectivity of the normative demand is an illusion, produced in us by our genes, for our own (and their) benefit.[26] But this view fails to meet the publicity standard just as Alexander and Wilson's views fail. If the source of the moral demand is an illusion produced by selective advantage, like an optical illusion produced in our visual apparatus, then this undercuts the force of the demand for advantage-blind choices or for justice in Scotus' sense.

There is some evidence of this effect in psychological literature. When people believe that psychological egoism is true, they are less inclined to be helpful to others. A before-and-after study was done on students enrolled in two introductory economics courses and an introductory astronomy course. The students were asked at the beginning and at the end of each course what they would do if they found an addressed envelope with $100 in it. I do not at all mean to insult my distinguished colleagues in economics, but while the students scored the same in the economics and astronomy courses at the beginning of the semester, the economics students were more willing to keep the money at the end. The difference probably resulted from exposure to the theory found pervasively in economics that motivation is fundamentally egoistic.[27] I speculate that the same would be true after a semester of Professor Ruse's philosophy course.

The Second and Third Strategies

I will mention the second and third strategies for dealing with the problem of the performance gap because I want to give you an idea of the scope of the analysis, but I will not try to discuss the details of these views. The second strategy is to keep the demand where it is, including the affection for justice, and then pretend that we are able by our own natural capacities to meet this demand. There are examples of this outside evolutionary ethics. For example, there is the view that it is only ignorance and lack of education that hold us back from being morally good, not some fundamental failure of the will. The Humanist Manifesto, published in 1933, stated that "[m]an is at last becoming aware that he alone is responsible for the realization of the world of his dreams, that he has within himself the power for its achievement."[28] This was just before the Second World War in which the people who carried out the massacres and holocaust were the most educated people in the world's history to that point. The Jews in the concentration camps had to perform Bach for their oppressors before they were put into the gas chambers. We have to ask whether the Humanist Manifesto was right, and whether it was supported by our experience of the world run by the people who believed it. There are also examples of this strategy, which I call "puffing up our capacities," within evolutionary ethics. Both Anthony O'Hear and Janet Richards propose that the affection for advantage is enough to take us to morality when it is added to our natural capacities for language and reason. Their idea is that reflection in itself carries with it a kind of distancing from our desires, and since we are by nature reflective beings, expressing our thoughts in universal concepts through language, we are led despite ourselves into an impartial moral perspective, adopting the aspiration to look at the world from the viewpoint of an ideal observer. [29] The trouble with this view is that reason and language are *not* sufficient, when added to the affection for advantage, to get us to the right ranking of the two affections for advantage and for justice. It is quite possible to be reflectively and rationally self-interested. The meticulous lists of holocaust victims kept by the Nazis suggest an exaggeration of reason, not a defect in it. The question here turns on what is meant by "reason." If we build the notion of morality into the notion of reason, then indeed reason will take us to morality. But this is a hollow victory, produced merely by re-definition. For then living by reason, or rationally, will no longer be merely a natural capacity, and there will be the same gap I have been describing all along but now labeled differently as the gap between our natural capacities and reason in this exalted sense.

The third strategy for dealing with the problem of the moral gap without bringing in God is to find a naturalistic substitute for God's assistance. An example outside evolutionary ethics is the Marxist view that our capacities for a good life will be changed if the proletariats take ownership of the means of production. Here is a substitute for God's assistance, something that will change our capacities so that they become adequate to the moral demand. Within evolutionary ethics, there are thinkers who want to make evolution itself the substitute for God's assistance. Some of the thinkers I have in mind would resist this description of what they are doing, because they are themselves theologians. They do not think of themselves as making evolution a *substitute* for God, but that is because they have made evolution God. They talk, like Philip Hefner, of God as the way things really are, and since they think the way things really are evolves, they talk about the evolution of God.[30] They think of God's transcendence as omnipresence, so that God transcends any part of the universe and any particular time in the universe, but not the universe in its spatial and temporal wholeness. Within this universe there is a direction of emergence, which produces its own ascent into higher and higher levels of life and consciousness. With this strategy we retain the traditional view of both the moral demand, which Hefner says is self-emptying love, and also of our natural biological tendency to prefer the self, which Hefner says is our sin of origin. So a moral gap remains, but defined now as a gap between morality and biology.

Then we postulate that there is this direction of emergence within the universe, what the Romantics in the nineteenth century called a life force, which is making possible first life itself, then higher forms of life, then finally culture and freedom. This view gives us a gradual synchronized rise of the moral demand and our cultural capacities linked together, to produce a kind of bio-social optimum. My problem with this view is that it does not take seriously enough the distinction between creature and creator. Scotus puts this in terms of God's existence being necessary and the universe being dependent, and so, possibly, non-existent. I think the resources for our salvation are located not within our freedom and culture, and not indeed within some internal force of evolution even if it is called "the evolution of God," but in the transcendent goodness of a God whose existence does not depend on the existence of anything else. But I am just stating my opinion at this point and not giving anything like a complete response, for that is beyond the scope of this presentation.

Conclusion

Let me try to tie some of the thoughts of this lecture together. The theory of evolution, I am claiming, cannot solve for us the problem of the moral gap. There are two gaps here: the affection gap between us and other animals, and the performance gap between our aspirations and the actual living of our lives. Human responsibility is located in this performance gap. We are responsible to live by the moral demand, but we do not seem to be able to do so by our own resources. Because of the affection gap between us and other animals, there is one answer to the problem of the moral gap we cannot give. We cannot explain our moral capacities by finding them already in non-human animals from which, according to the theory of evolution, we evolved. But would we learn anything useful about human morality *if* the theory of evolution were true in its application to human beings? We would learn something about the raw material, so to speak, on which God's assistance works. We would learn more detail about what our natural capacities are, or, in Scotus' term, we would learn more about the affection for advantage.

But if evolution were proposed as a substitute source of the moral demand, we would be in danger of losing both morality and responsibility. Why is this? Because we would end up reducing the demand in one of the ways I have described, and if we lower the demand we also lower our accountability or moral responsibility along with it.

I want to end with one more thought. What does Christian scholarship contribute? I can now use my own discipline as an example. Christian moral philosophy can help us in one way by contributing to an understanding of the moral gap. If I have been right, we need an account of how the moral gap might be bridged which does not either lower the demand or exaggerate our natural capacities, and we need a theory of the source of the moral demand which passes the publicity standard. Christianity has some resources here and this is not surprising, for Western morality has its roots deep in Christian doctrine, though not only there. If we try to detach or un-moor or uproot ourselves from this doctrine, we should expect certain kinds of incoherence to result. For example, we will lose the traditional answers to the two questions, "Can we be morally good?" and "Why should we be morally good?" and it will be hard to find a substitute. Christian moral philosophy has as one of its tasks to uncover this kind of incoherence, and point us to a retrieval of the resources for overcoming it.

---

[1] John Calvin, *Institutes of the Christian Religion,* trans. Ford Lewis Battles, ed. John T. McNeill, The Library of Christian Classics, vol. 21 (Philadelphia: Westminster Press, 1960), 3.23.2.

[2] Immanuel Kant, *Critique of Practical Reason,* trans. Mary Gregor (Cambridge: Cambridge University Press, 1997), 5.158.

[3] Augustine, *Grace and Free Will,* chapter 32, in *Basic Writings of Saint Augustine,* ed. Whitney J. Oates, vol. 1, A Select Library of the Nicene and Post-Nicene Fathers of the Christian Church, ed. Philip Schaff (New York: Random House, 1948), 759.

[4] Martin Luther, *The Bondage of the Will,* trans. J.I. Packer and O.R. Johnston (London: James Clarke & Co. Ltd., 1957), 152.

[5] See Richard B. Brandt, *Ethical Theory: The Problems of Normative and Critical Ethics* (Englewood Cliffs, NJ: Prentice-Hall, 1959) and R.M. Hare, *Moral Thinking: Its Levels, Method, and Point* (Oxford: Clarendon Press, 1981).

[6] Charles Darwin, *The Origin of Species By Means of Natural Selection or The Preservation of Favoured Races in the Struggle for Life* (1859; reprint, New York: Bantam Books, 1999), 167.

[7] Isaac Watts, "Song XX: Against Idleness and Mischief," in *Divine Songs for the Use of Children* (New Haven: Sidney's Press, 1817), 37.

[8] Darwin, *Origin,* 195.

[9] Edward O. Wilson, *Sociobiology: The New Synthesis* (Cambridge, MA: The Belknap Press of Harvard University Press, 1975).

[10] See John Cartwright, *Evolution and Human Behavior: Darwinian Perspectives on Human Nature* (Cambridge, MA: The MIT Press, 2000), 87-88.

[11] Plato, *Republic,* 334b.

[12] Plato, *Crito,* 49a-e; Plato, *Gorgias,* 508b-509c.

[13] Frans de Waal, *Good Natured: The Origins of Right and Wrong in Humans and Other Animals* (Cambridge, MA: Harvard University Press, 1996), 91-92.

[14] Larry Arnhart, *Darwinian Natural Right: The Biological Ethics of Human Nature* (Albany, NY: State University of New York Press, 1998), 17, 30.

[15] Arnhart, 36.

[16] Arnhart, 29-36.

[17] Charles Darwin, *The Descent of Man* (London: John Murray, 1871), 1: 101, quoted in Arnhart, 144.

[18] Arnhart, 146-147.

[19] Arnhart, 149.

[20] Arnhart, 149.

[21] See Nel Noddings, *Caring: A Feminine Approach to Ethics and Moral Education* (Berkeley and Los Angeles: University of California Press, 1984), 86.

[22] Richard D. Alexander, *Darwinism and Human Affairs* (Seattle: University of Washington Press, 1979).

[23] Richard D. Alexander and Andrew F. Richards, "Group-Living, Conflicts of Interest, and the Concept of God" (photocopy), chap. 24, pp. 12, 15.

[24] Alexander and Richards, chap. 24, p. 5.

[25] David Sloan Wilson, "Church as Organism" (photocopy), chap. 3.

[26] Michael Ruse, *Can a Darwinian be a Christian? The Relationship between Science and Religion* (Cambridge: Cambridge University Press, 2001).

[27] Robert H. Frank, Thomas Gilovich, and Dennis T. Regan, "Does Studying Economics Inhibit Cooperation?" *Journal of Economic Perspectives* 7, no. 2 (1993): 168-170.

[28] J. A. C. Fagginer Auer, et al., *Humanist Manifesto I* (Buffalo, NY: Prometheus Books, 1973), 10. First published in *The New Humanist* 6, no. 3 (1933).

[29] See Anthony O'Hear, *Beyond Evolution: Human Nature and the Limits of Evolutionary Explanation* (Oxford: Clarendon Press, 1997) and Janet Radcliffe Richards, *Human Nature after Darwin: A Philosophical Introduction* (London: Routledge, 2000).

[30] Philip Hefner, *The Human Factor: Evolution, Culture, and Religion* (Minneapolis: Fortress Press, 1993).

Christian Scholarship and the Practice of Science

John Polkinghorne

Let me say first of all that it is very good to be at Calvin College again; I always enjoy being here, and I am grateful for the invitation to give a lecture this evening. I'd also like to say that it is good and indeed, in a way, a privilege to be in the United States at this time. All of us in Britain were deeply shocked and saddened by the events of the eleventh of September, and the American people and your leaders have been in our thoughts and prayers since that time.

The Restrictions of Science

My topic tonight is Christian Scholarship and the practice of science and by "science" I mean natural science, the investigation of the structure and history of the physical world and of biological life within that world. I am bracketing out the human sciences from consideration on this occasion. Their complexity and their centrality to theological discourse raise very different questions from those that I am able to discuss now. I understand science, in the sense in which I have just described it, to be circumscribed by two restrictions that define its nature, enable its success, and limit the scope of the significance of its discoveries.

The first limitation is that the motivation for science's beliefs derives from its encounter with the world treated solely as an object, an "it" that can be manipulated and put to the experimental test as the investigator pleases. The experimental method is science's great secret weapon, the source both of its triumphs and also of the confines of its relevance. Even those sciences, such as cosmology and evolutionary biology, that seek to survey an historical process, much of which is not directly accessible to us, depend heavily on the insights of experimental sciences, such as physics and genetics, in order to make sense of the phenomena that they interpret as evidence of past events.

The second limitation is in terms of what are treated as acceptable grounds of explanation. Science speaks only in terms of efficient causes and does not appeal directly to other forms of explanation, such as the teleological or the axiological. Purpose and value are excluded from the official vocabulary that science employs to present and defend its conclusions.

I take both these limitations simply to be matters of methodological expediency. Limiting the field of vision brings a narrow set of issues into sharp focus. One cannot doubt that Galileo's advice to concentrate on what he considered to be the primary quantities of matter and motion, and to set aside the so-called secondary qualities of human sensual perception, led to an extremely successful program of discovery. But what has proved to be an excellent heuristic technique would become ontologically disastrous if it were mistaken for the provision of an adequate basis for metaphysical conclusions. The lunar landscape to which science restricts its attention is a cold abstraction from reality. The success of its impersonal account holds only in a limited domain, and that success by no means leads to the preposterous conclusion that personal experience is just an epiphenomenon of little intrinsic importance. Music is much more than neural response to vibrations in the air, though that is all that an implausible scientism could say about it. Science's reliance on the experimentally repeatable carries no implication that there is not a different kind of significance to be found in the unique.

The Reason for Scientific Research

Let me go on to ask why people devote their lives to pure scientific research. As with any other worthwhile activity, there is much routine, weary labor, and frustration involved. I was a theoretical physicist, and at the end of the average working day my waste paper basket contained a number of crumpled pieces of paper as the "good ideas" of the morning proved less persuasive following further reflection in the afternoon. My experimental colleagues would tell me stories of their struggles to get recalcitrant pieces of apparatus to work in the way expected of them. There is a lot of struggle involved in the practice of science. So why do we do it?

We do it because we want to *understand* the physical world. The reward for all the effort involved is the sense of wonder that comes with each new insight into the marvelous workings of the universe. Notice that I am talking about pure science. Of course, science's lusty offspring, technology, also enables us to get things done, and all our lives have been enriched in countless ways by the inventions that have resulted from technology. Yet pragmatic success is not the main driving force of science itself. To get the point, consider a little parable that I have used before, but which I hope will bear repetition.

One day a black box is delivered at the Meteorological Office with the following instructions: Feed in details of today's weather through slot A, turn the handle, and a perfect forecast of the weather in a week's time will emerge from slot B. It all seems rather unlikely, but they are broad-minded people at the Met Office, so they give it a go. Lo and behold, it works! If meteorology was simply about weather forecasting, about getting things done, the task of the Met Office could now be perfectly fulfilled by the use of this mysterious machine. The meteorologists could all go home, just leaving one colleague behind to turn the handle each day. Do you think they would all depart? Of course not! Very soon the scientists would be dismantling that black box in the effort to find out how it worked. Meteorologists do not only want to predict the weather; above all they want to *understand* it.

Understanding the Physical World

So how does science set about the task of gaining understanding of the physical world? That is a philosophical question, and the twentieth century saw great activity in the philosophy of science. I do not think it could be said, however, that many widely agreed upon conclusions emerged, either about the nature of the scientific method or about the character of its attainments. Clearly involved are both an appeal to experience and recourse to a theoretical framework of understanding, but the fact that significant scientific evidence is always *interpreted* evidence means that experiment and theory intertwine in subtle ways. This means that the evaluation of what is going on cannot be reduced to ticking off a checklist or following an algorithmic procedure that simply confronts pure theoretical prediction with pure experimental results. Michael Polanyi, who knew science from the inside, having been a distinguished physical chemist before he turned to philosophy, has made it clear that acts of personal judgment are fundamental to the practice of science, which also requires prior commitment to a chosen but corrigible point of view.[1] Yet, the long-term fruitfulness of well-winnowed scientific ideas, often predicting or interpreting phenomena not taken into account in the initial framing of a theory, is powerfully persuasive that scientists are on to something, that they are gaining a verisimilitudinous account of the way things are. However, the occasional radical revisions necessary when new regimes of experience are first explored show that science falls short of attaining absolute and exhaustive truth about the physical world. Scientists make maps of reality, accurate on an appropriate scale, but not capable of giving a total account of the terrain.

The point of view about science that I have sketched so briefly is one that may be called *critical realism* – "critical" because recognition of the role of judgment and commitment in the practice of science acknowledges that a certain precariousness is involved in reaching conclusions that fall short of logical necessity, but "realism" because the fruitfulness of scientific ideas persuades us nevertheless that they give us a tightening grip on an actual reality.

Of course, there is much contention about these questions, but there can be no doubt that critical realism is the stance adopted, consciously or unconsciously, by the vast majority of working scientists. Why would we do science unless we believed that we were learning what the physical world is like? And how could technology succeed so well unless the science on which it relies was not a good approximation to the way things are? The practice of science has about it an undeniable feel of discovery as, time and again, nature resists our prior expectation and drives us on to understandings more powerful and more profound than we could ever have anticipated on our own. I think this first order testimony of the scientists should be taken with great seriousness in the second order reflections of the philosophers of science.

The Role of Christian Scholarship

So where does Christian scholarship come into all this? My answer in a nutshell is, "obliquely but fundamentally." I say "obliquely" because I believe that science, acting within its self-restricted domain of enquiry and following its limited strategies of explanation, is essentially a self-contained activity and is not in need of direct assistance from any other intellectual discipline. I do not believe that there is a distinctive "Christian physics," or even a distinctive "Christian biology." I am able to say this because of my restriction to the natural sciences and my bracketing the human sciences out of present consideration. It seems clear to me that it does make sense to talk of a "Christian anthropology," because the issues involved in discussing human nature are so much more complex and multi-dimensional than those arising from natural science, and they demand a discourse that is rich and many-layered in its character.

I assert science's self-containment for two reasons. One is simply the observational fact that scientists of the highest distinction may be religious believers drawn from any of the world faith traditions, or they may be people of no religious belief at all. It is easy to point to Nobel Prize winners who are Jewish, Christian, Moslem, agnostic, or atheist. I do not see that these differences in religious belief correlate in any way with access to scientific insight. My second reason is that the lessons of history strongly suggest that there is every reason to suppose that scientifically posable questions may be expected to receive scientifically stateable answers, however difficult these answers may sometimes be to find. Currently, we do not know the biochemical pathways by which life first came to be here on planet Earth, but I think it would be rash indeed to suppose that people will never be able to attain that knowledge. Putting the matter theologically, the one "god" who is well and truly dead is the god of the gaps. No one should shed a tear for his passing, for he was only a pseudo-deity – which is why I do not feel any sensitivity about which pronoun to use to refer to him. The god of the gaps, appealed to as the explanation of last resort in relation to physical or biological process, was just a bad theological mistake. The Creator does not lurk in the murky and understood parts of the universe, for the true God is the God of the whole cosmic show, the One who holds in being all that is. The reliable laws of nature, to which science appeals as the ground of its explanation, are pale reflections of the faithfulness of the Creator. The god of the gaps, on the other hand, was a kind of Cheshire cat deity, perpetually fading away with the advance of knowledge, always over the next intellectual horizon.

How then does Christian scholarship impinge upon the practice of science? Not as a secret source of knowledge, a kind of ace of trumps that the Holy Spirit has kindly put up the sleeve of the believing scientist, but, as I have already said, obliquely yet fundamentally. Although scientific questions may be expected to receive scientific answers, we have every reason to believe that there are many questions, both meaningful and necessary to ask, that are not scientific in character and whose answers will, therefore, have to be sought from other sources. Some of these questions relate, obliquely yet fundamentally, to the practice of science itself. It is my conviction that Christian belief provides the most persuasive and extensive basis for their answering.

The Wider Context of Intelligibility

There are three ways in which Christian scholarship can fulfill this role. The first is to provide a *wider context of intelligibility*. Those imbued with a thirst for understanding will not find that thirst quenched by science alone. Interestingly enough, some of these further questions that press upon us arise from our experience of the practice of science itself, but they fall outside the ambit of scientific explanation. They are metaquestions, going beyond the purely scientific. I would like to briefly draw attention to two such questions to which, I believe, Christian scholarship can provide particularly illuminating responses.

One is simply *Why is science possible at all?* Of course, the necessities of biological survival can explain why human beings have developed a capacity to make sense of our immediate experience of the environment in which we live. If we could not make generalizations such as "It is a bad idea to walk off the top of a high cliff," we would not be around for very long. But it does not follow from this that people like Isaac Newton and Albert Einstein can come along and, by great creative leaps of scientific intuition, see that the force that makes the cliff so dangerous is only an aspect of a universal gravity that also controls the motions of the planets and the structure of the whole cosmos. Human ability to understand the counterintuitive realms of quantum physics and of curved cosmic space cannot plausibly be thought of as just a happy accidental spin-off from much more mundane necessities. The universe is astonishingly rationally transparent to scientific enquiry on all scales of its being. Moreover, the universe is also strikingly rationally beautiful. Invariably, physicists find that the equations that describe the fundamental laws of nature possess the unmistakable character of mathematical beauty. Instinctively they feel that an ugly equation must have something wrong with it because it runs counter to this deep and repeated experience. The use of abstract mathematics to guide physical thought in this way is no mere act of aesthetic indulgence, for we have found time and again that it is only "beautiful" theories of this kind that prove to have the long-term fruitfulness that persuades us of their verisimilitude.

The transparent beauty of fundamental physics is the source of that wonder that is the reward for all the labors of scientific research. It provides a powerful incentive, for which the physicist is grateful, and a powerful aid to discovery, which the physicist is only too happy to exploit. Yet, viewed from within the limited discourse of science itself, these basic aspects of scientific practice appear simply to be fortunate accidents that one enjoys without knowing why they are the case. Einstein once made the well-known remark that, in his view, the only incomprehensible thing about the universe is that it is comprehensible. A person endowed with any degree of intellectual curiosity must go on to ask the metaquestion, Why is science possible in this way that goes so far beyond everyday necessity? Another Nobel Prize winning physicist, Eugene Wigner, spoke of "the unreasonable effectiveness of mathematics" when he considered the way in which it opens up for us the secrets of the universe.[2] Wigner considered this a gift that we "neither understand nor deserve."[3]

The Christian scholar has access to a deeper source of intelligibility that makes sense of these remarkable scientific experiences. The rational beauty of a universe shot through, as it were, with signs of mind becomes understandable because there is indeed the Mind of its Creator behind the wonder of cosmic order. We are able to discover that order because we are creatures made in the image of our Creator. I believe that the possibility of science is part of the deposit of the *imago dei*.

The second metaquestion to consider is, Why is the universe so special? Here I am referring to the surprising collection of scientific insights gathered together under the rubric of the Anthropic Principle. Although, as far as we know, life only began when the universe was about fifteen billion years old, and self-conscious life when it was eleven billion years old, there is a real sense in which the cosmos was pregnant with carbon-based life from the very beginning. I say that because the cosmic physical fabric – the given laws of nature that control the basic forces at work in the world – had to take a very specific, "finely-tuned," form if life as we know it was to be a possibility at all. I shall not rehearse the often-discussed and well-known considerations that persuade us that this is so. It will be sufficient to catch their flavor by noting that there could be no carbon-based life unless there was carbon in the world, that the only place in the universe where carbon can be made is in the interi-or nuclear furnaces of the stars, and that the process by which this happens is dependent in a very sensitive way on the actual strengths of the nuclear forces involved. Similar considerations relate to the many other chemical elements that are the raw materials of life (other than hydrogen). They are all made in the stars by a delicately balanced chain of nuclear reactions. All living beings are creatures made of stardust.

Many scientists were upset by the thought that there was something spe-cial about our universe. Their professional instinct is to prefer the general to the particular, and so they would have liked to believe that our world was just a common or garden specimen of what a universe might be like. In an attempt to defuse the issue, some have supposed that there is, in fact, a vast portfolio of other existing universes, all with different laws of nature and all unobserv-able by us. The fact that our world is hospitable to life is then to be thought of as just a chance event, as if it corresponded fortuitously to the winning tick-et drawn in a gigantic cosmic lottery. This idea is a metaphysical speculation of breathtaking prodigality. The Christian scholar has access to a more eco-nomical explanation. For us the universe is not just "any old world," but it is a creation. There is then no perplexity in its having been endowed by its Creator with those finely-tuned laws and circumstances that have allowed it to have a fruitful, life-generating history.

I am a passionate believer in the unity of knowledge and in the value of seeking as comprehensive and integrated an understanding as possible of the rich reality within which we live. Colleges and universities can be understood as being the institutional expressions of these convictions. Christian scholar-ship has an important and indispensable place within the academic world just because it offers an attractive way of achieving this kind of metaphysical wholeness. Its ability to take aspects of experience arising from the practice of science, in the way we have discussed, which might on a narrow view be seen as no more than amazingly happy accidents, and to make them fully intelligi-ble within the wider context of understanding provided by Christian theolo-gy, establishes its right to be part of the Academy.

The Endorsement of Value

Central to all metaphysical discussion is the question of the breadth and inclusiveness of the account of reality that is being offered. Facile schemes that try to fit the richness of experience into the narrow bed of an oversimplified theory by Procrustean truncation are of no value at all. The second way in which Christian scholarship impacts, obliquely yet fundamentally, the prac-tice of science is through the *endorsement of value*. At first sight, this claim might seem strange. After all, it is conventional to say that science is "value-free." But what that means is simply that direct appeal to axiological argument is excluded from the self-limited domain of scientific justification. The editors of *The Physical Review* would not accept a paper proposing a new theory of particle physics that simply claimed that it was right because this is the way things ought to be. The official published discourse of science is certainly value-free in this narrow sense, but that is not at all the case when we come to consider the informal conversations of scientists that precede the formalized act of submitting results to a learned journal. I have already drawn attention to the way in which mathematical beauty functions as a heuristic guide to physical discovery. A theoretical physicist happy enough to have hit on a beautiful equation will often express the conviction that this must be the right way to think, long before final experimental endorsement is available. So natural is this supposition that colleagues are very likely to be disposed to agree. Judgments of this kind do not invariably prove to be correct, but they are vindicated in an impressive proportion of cases.

Einstein had the essential physical idea on which his general theory of relativity is based by 1907. He then had to find the right way to formulate it, and it took him an eight-year search, ending in November 1915, before he hit on an appropriately beautiful equation to express what he had in mind. Once he had the equation, he had to set to work to calculate whether it would resolve a long-known discrepancy between Newtonian prediction and the actual behavior of the planet Mercury. In fact it did so, but I feel sure that Einstein already believed he had made a big discovery simply on the basis of the presence of mathematical beauty. In those branches of science less totally mathematized than fundamental physics, a similar role in inducing conviction is played by the value-laden characteristics of elegance and economy.

The contrast between the value-free style of official announcements and the value-based way in which discoveries are actually made, is part of Polanyi's point that scientific practice is irreducibly an activity of persons.[4] When we consider the fifteen-billion-year history of cosmic process, perhaps the most remarkable event that we know about is the emergence of self-conscious persons here on planet Earth. In humanity, the universe has become aware of itself. Pascal said of human beings that we are just reeds, frail creatures set in the immensity of the universe that surrounds us, but we are *thinking* reeds and that makes us greater than all the stars, for we know them and ourselves and they know nothing.[5]

Christian scholarship endorses the significance of the personal and the reality of value. Human beings live in a multi-layered world, which is not only the location of physical events but also the arena of moral choice, the carrier of beauty, and the place of encounter with the presence of the sacred. This is so because this world is the creation of the God who is the origin and ground of the good, the true, and the beautiful. Value is as real as matter and energy; the subjective is at least as significant as the objective; the unique is to be taken with quite as much seriousness as the repeatable. The theological meta-physics of Christian belief has the breadth and comprehensiveness in its account of reality to enable it to be a credible basis for understanding the rich-ness of human experience.

Ethical Applications

Moral values are important for the enterprise of science. Its successful prac-tice depends upon the truthful reporting of results and ideas and upon a gen-erous attitude toward the sharing of knowledge and insight. Plagiarism or fal-sification is rightly fatal to a scientific career, and its occurrence is commend-ably rare in the scientific community. Of course, Christian scholars will be happy to be a part of this ethical practice and to make common cause with other colleagues in maintaining these high standards of conduct. But there is a further important aspect to be considered. Christian scholarship can make its third contribution to the practice of science by the insights it can offer into the *ethical applications of scientific discoveries.*

Pure science gives us knowledge of the workings of the physical world and of the biological processes of life. Technology then takes that knowledge and turns it into power to manipulate the world and so to bring about a great vari-ety of human purposes. However, not everything that can be done should be done. If we are to make the right use of these gifts of knowledge and power, we shall have to add to them a third gift, namely wisdom to choose the good and to refuse the bad. I do not need to emphasize the pressing questions that confront scientists and technologists today as they consider the uses to which their discoveries might be put. These problems are intensified by the current rapid rate of scientific advance. Nowhere is this more clearly exemplified today than in the field of genetics, where our ambiguous power to intervene in the inter-generational processes of life offers both the promise of the cure for severe congenital disease and also the threatening prospect of unaccept-able eugenic manipulation of human beings.

But where shall wisdom be found? The answer given in the Book of Job is "Behold, the fear of the Lord, that is wisdom; and to depart from evil is under-standing" (Job 28:28 King James Version). The religious traditions are great reservoirs of wisdom, and Christian scholarship will certainly have a signifi-cant contribution to make to the discussion of the ethical uses of the fruits of science and technology.

It so happens that for the last twelve years or so I have been involved in Britain in the consideration of questions of this kind, mostly in the field of genetics. Part of this activity has been in a church-based setting, where I have been until recently the chairman of the Church of England's Science, Medicine, and Technology Committee. But the greater part of the work has been on behalf of the British Government as a member, and quite often the chairman, of a variety of committees charged with considering particular issues and sometimes required to formulate appropriate codes of practice. Perhaps I may comment briefly on what I have learned from this experience.

The work of a committee of this kind usually takes place in two distinct phases. In the first phase, the committee is exploring the scientific and technical basis of the matter in hand. One has to know what actions are possible and what their consequences are expected to be. At this stage, the members of the committee who are the experts take the lead in the discussions. The rest of us (and, as a theoretical physicist on a committee dealing with genetics, I am definitely in the non-expert camp) have to listen and take in as much as we can of what we are being told. Knowledge is a much better basis for decision than ignorance and so the available scientific and technical insight is much to be welcomed. My impression has been that my expert colleagues were genuinely concerned to "tell it like it is" in a way that was scrupulous and free from hidden agendas.

A second phase then follows. One knows what might be done, but should it be done? The character of the committee now changes. No longer is it a dual community of experts and non-experts; it becomes a single community of moral beings in search of ethically correct conclusions. I have been impressed – and often relieved – that there is a way in which people of good will can work together to form a consensus about the right way forward. If there is any difference between expert and non-expert at this stage, it is that the latter are free from the danger of being influenced by what one might call the "technological imperative," the way in which the excitement of research can tend to push the scientist in the direction of simply carrying on. "We've done this and then that, so why not do the next thing?" One of the reasons why decisions in these matter cannot simply be left to the experts is the need to keep before them the question of whether the next step is the right step.

Christian Contributions

Is there a distinctive Christian contribution that in practical terms can be made to this process or, in more academic terms, that can be resourced by Christian scholarship? I think that there is, but it is often of a subtle, or even tacit, kind. Note the sort of questions being considered: Should insurance companies have access to the results of genetic tests for congenital diseases not yet manifesting clinically detectable symptoms? Is it right to seek to cure severe diseases by using cell nuclear replacement techniques that provide tissue generated from stem cells that are immunologically compatible with the recipient, but which have been derived by an embryonic route? These are not questions whose answers can be found in the pages of scripture or easily correlated with what we do find there. The same could be said about the appeal to the ethical discussions found in the prior Christian tradition. The difficult problems are ones that our generation faces for the first time, and that is why committed and responsible Christians will not always find it easy to agree on what the answers should be.

Nevertheless, there are, I believe, two ways in which Christian understanding has a significant contribution to make. We do not have a monopoly on ethical principles and insight. Many persons who are not religious at all will believe with us, for instance, that human beings are always to be treated as ends and never merely as means. They will agree with us that humanity has a duty of care and respect for other living beings and for the environment of the Earth, which is our common home. If there is a difference between us, and I think that there is, it lies in Christians having the firmest possible grounds for these convictions. The ultimate reason why every individual human being is of the highest moral significance is because each of us is loved and valued by our heavenly Father. The Earth and its living inhabitants are to be respected because they are part of God's creation and not part of our own possessions. The very moral principles that these beliefs express are neither disguised survival strategies nor socially useful conventions, but they are intimations of the good and perfect will of the Creator.

The second Christian contribution to these ethical discussions requires particularly careful statement, since it can easily become distorted in ways that are destructive rather than constructive. Much of our ethical perplexity arises from situations in which different moral principles seem to point us in conflicting directions. Recently in Britain, we had a case in which two Siamese twins were so joined together that they could not be expected to live more than a few months in that configuration, yet to separate them would inevitably cause the immediate death of the weaker twin, who had no heart or lungs of her own. It might seem better that one twin should live instead of both dying, but the doctors felt great moral unease at taking steps that would directly be the cause of the death of one of the twins. It is understandable that there was much anguish and disagreement about what should be done. In the grey world of actual ethical decisions there is often no unequivocally good outcome possible. Putting it another way, there are frequently problems that have no full solution. We live in an age with a great emphasis on present fulfillment. Much contemporary thinking finds it difficult to accept that there are situations that are irreducibly problematic. It is felt that there must be a solution, and it is to science that people often look to find the missing magic. They feel correspondingly resentful when the reality of the situation means that the desired solution is not forthcoming. I hope I will not sound unsympathetic to couples who suffer the real bereavement of being unable to have their own children, but there must be some limits set to what are ethically acceptable ways of trying to deal with infertility.

Not every problem can have a solution. It seems to me that the Christian eschatological hope of an ultimate fulfillment of God's purposes in the life of the new creation makes it a little easier for us to realistically face some of these unpalatable facts and the very difficult situations that they give rise to. You will understand why I feel nervous about saying this, for it can so easily slide into a callous acceptance of present suffering – particularly in the lives of others – dismissed on the basis of a facile pie-in-the-sky argument. Nevertheless, I feel that something like this has to be said. A rather blunt way of putting it would be to say that the Christian seeks to care for life and to preserve it, but also knows that death is not the worst thing that can ever happen.

Let me summarize what I have said so far. I have suggested that Christian scholarship is essentially neutral with respect to the professional practice of science in the course of the latter's search for understanding, conducted on its own terms and within its self-limited domain of relevance. Yet theological insight offers the prospect of locating science's remarkable successes within a more profound context of intelligibility, of describing a wider setting for understanding and humane experience to which science itself contributes only a part, and of undergirding the quest by persons of good will for right decisions about the ethical uses of the discoveries of science and technology.

While I see Christian thinking as neutral with respect to the pursuit of science – so that believer and unbeliever alike operate in the same way in physics or biology – I certainly do not think that Christian thinking is neutral about the undertaking of the enterprise of science. Quite the contrary, for it seems to me that Christian scholarship must be strongly supportive of the scientific enterprise. The reason is simple enough. Christians are seeking to be servants of the God of truth. Therefore, we must affirm and welcome all aspects of the truth, from wherever they may come. Science certainly does not possess anything like the whole truth. The scientistic claim to the contrary presents us with a picture of reality that is stunted, lifeless, and desperately implausible in the poverty of the account that it is able to give. Yet science certainly does give us access to some of the truth, particularly about the pattern and history of the universe in which we live. This we must gladly accept, treating it with respect and seriousness.

Of course, there will be puzzles and challenges concerning how these scientific bits of truth relate to other bits of truth that we possess, including the truths of the Christian revelation. I do not need to spell out for you how this has been the case in the course of intellectual history, sometimes with considerable intensity of feeling on the part of those involved. These experiences are just the counterparts in metaphysical discourse of the unresolved discrepancies from which science itself is never wholly free. The pursuit of truth is not easy and it will always have its difficulties. Those of us who believe that the Lord our God is one Lord, and that the Holy Spirit is the spirit of truth, can join in that pursuit with confidence in its value and in its ultimate success.

Christian Scholarship and the Christian Community

Christian scholarship has an important role to play here in relation to the whole Christian community. Those who are both learned and faithful have to be able to show that there is no need for the Christian ever to fear science. Rather there should be a welcome for the truths it conveys. To use a venerable way of putting the matter, we need to read both divine books, the book of scripture and the book of nature. Sometimes our reading may encounter perplexities, and there may well be the need for revisions of our understandings in both science and theology, but in the end our faith in the one true God will assure us of the ultimate unity of knowledge and of success in the search for truth.

Trust in honest and open learning has often been powerfully expressed in the Thomist tradition of Christian thought. One of my favorite quotations is drawn from the writing of a great twentieth century Thomist, the Canadian Jesuit, Bernard Lonergan. He once wrote that "God is the *unrestricted* act of understanding, the eternal rapture glimpsed in every Archimedean cry of Eureka" [italics added].[6] Those words are the charter of the intellectual liberty of the Christian man and woman.

Two other great figures of Christian thought can be called on as witnesses to the role of science in the enterprise of Christian scholarship. One is St. Augustine. You will recall that one of the first reasons Augustine questioned the Manichean belief to which he had been an adherent for ten years arose from the antiseptic effects of scientific insight. His doubts were raised when he observed that contemporary astronomers were much more accurate than the Manichean sages in predicting eclipses. Later on, the Christian Augustine was to say that when there seemed to be a clash between science and scripture, one should be prepared to reconsider the interpretation of the relevant scriptural passage. Galileo was to call this wise advice in his own defense more than twelve centuries later.

My second witness is no less a person than John Calvin himself. He seems to have been the Reformer with the clearest appreciation of the value of the nascent science of his day. (The remark often attributed to him, "Who will put the authority of Copernicus above that of the Holy Spirit?" is a nineteenth century fabrication.)[7] Calvin's doctrine of the accommodation of Scripture's manner of expression to the common perceptions of humankind enabled him to accept without difficulty the conclusions of contemporary astronomers. He said that "Moses wrote in a popular style" and adapted his language in accordance with common experience. The Bible was not written as the definitive word on abstruse sciences but as a book for laypeople.[8]

On a more personal note, I feel only gratitude for the twenty-five years that I was able to spend working as a theoretical elementary particle physicist. I regarded it as being a Christian vocation to use such talents as I had in this way. I always want to emphasize that I did not leave physics because I was in any way disillusioned with science. I simply felt that I had done my little bit in that area and so the time had come to do something else. I suppose that the last twenty years I have spent working at the interface between science and theology might seem to have been more explicitly concerned with Christian scholarship, but I believe that both these periods of my adult activity have equally been part of the attempt to serve the God of truth.

Science is a proper part of Christian scholarship, a fact to which the existence of excellent departments of science in many Christian colleges here in North America bears witness. Perhaps I may allow myself, as a friendly bystander, to make some brief comments on your Christian college system. At first sight, it seems strange to a contemporary visitor from Britain to find university institutions that have an explicit confessional basis. Of course, our ancient universities were originally founded with explicit ecclesiastical roots and my own University of Cambridge still has "religion" as one of its statutory pursuits, alongside "learning and research." However, our conception of the nature of free academic enquiry means that for more than a century no British university has imposed confessional requirements on either staff or students. Personally, I would not wish for it to be any different.

What then do I make of a Christian college such as Calvin? Through fruitful acquaintance I have come to see that institutions of this kind have their own particular value. I locate this especially in a two-fold witness that they make. First, the Christian college stands as a witness to the Church, through the scrupulous standards of its academic excellence, of the paramount importance to the Christian community of the search for truth. Second, the Christian college stands also as a witness to the Academy, through its acknowledgement and nurturing of the authentic standards of the religious life, of the paramount importance for the human search for truth and the acknowledgement of the transcendent reality of God. It has been a great privilege to take part in this conference and to honor the one hundred and twenty-five year pursuit of Christian scholarship that has taken place here. I pray God's blessing on the many years that lie ahead for Calvin College.

---

1 Michael Polanyi, *Personal Knowledge: Towards a Post-Critical Philosophy* (London: Routledge & Kegan Paul, 1958).

2 Eugene P. Wigner, "The Unreasonable Effectiveness of Mathematics in the Natural Sciences," *Communications on Pure and Applied Mathematics* 13, no. 1 (1960): 1-14.

3 Wigner, 14.

4 See Polanyi, *Personal Knowledge.*

5 See Blaise Pascal, *Pascal's Pensées*, trans. H.F. Stewart (New York: Pantheon Books, 1965), 83.

6 Bernard Lonergan, *Insight: A Study of Human Understanding* (New York: Philosophical Library; London: Longmans, 1958), 684.

7 Dennis Alexander, *Rebuilding the Matrix* (Oxford: Lion Publishing, 2001), 129.

8 John Calvin, *Commentary on the First Book of Moses called Genesis*, vol. 1, trans. John King (Grand Rapids: Wm. B. Eerdmans, 1948), 86. See also his note on Psalm 136:7 in the *Commentary on the Book of Psalms*, trans. James Anderson (Grand Rapids: Wm. B. Eerdmans, 1949) 5:184-5: "The Holy Spirit had no intention to teach

astronomy; and, in proposing instruction meant to be common to the simplest and most uneducated persons, he made use by Moses and the other Prophets of popular language, that none might shelter himself under the pretext of obscurity…. [T]he Holy Spirit would rather speak childishly than unintelligibly to the humble and unlearned."

Christian Scholarship and the Changing Center of World Christianity

Tite Tiénou

I would like to salute the friends, faculty, and colleagues at Calvin College for their foresight in planning a conference on Christian scholarship at a time when our world desperately needs direction. I have particularly puzzled over the title of the conference as it is stated in the publicity: "Christian Scholarship . . . *for What?*" This title takes on special significance in my mind because of our present need for answers to a multitude of questions in the world today. At times like these, we are reminded that scholarship, especially Christian scholarship, cannot and must not be pursued in isolation from the wider context of community.

For Christians today, that wider community is, indeed, *ever* wider. As I see it, my assignment is to help lift our eyes to the wider Christian community beyond Grand Rapids, beyond Michigan, and beyond the United States of America. I will do so in three steps. I will first present a brief sketch of my convictions regarding Christian scholarship. Then I will remind us of the status of contemporary Christianity. Thirdly, and finally, I want to direct our attention to the challenges of making Christian scholarship an endeavor in which Christian scholars from the world community participate fully.

Christian Scholarship for Comprehensive Discipleship and Witness

I begin this essay with a brief word on my convictions regarding Christian scholarship. I will not take time to articulate the nature and purposes of Christian scholarship. Others have done this ably either here in this conference or in print. Rather, I offer the following convictions for the sake of clarity. For me, Christian scholarship is distinct from its non-Christian counterpart by the fact that it is rooted in the scholar's relationship to God, who is Father, Son, and Holy Spirit. This relationship is the beginning and the foundation of Christian scholarship. It is what James Sire calls an "attitude."[1] This attitude, expressed in Proverbs 1:7 as "The fear of the Lord is the beginning of knowledge" (New Revised Standard Version), is essentially a recognition of the self in relationship to God. This recognition is reflected in humility and is the principal building block of the Christian mind. Humility makes us ever mindful that all human knowledge is approximate and tentative.

Since the Christian mind begins with such an attitude and calls for humility, it means that scholars demonstrate humility when they acknowledge the fact that the increase of knowledge and the maturation of scholarship require community. You are not surprised that a person from a continent known for its emphasis on community should call attention to the community dimension of scholarship. But I do not do so just for African reasons. I emphasize community more for Christian and scholarly reasons. Christian life requires participation in a community of disciples.[2] Likewise, professional societies (communities of peers) are essential for the advancement of scholarship.

For me, then, Christian scholarship begins with an attitude. It is rooted in "the fear of the Lord" and its purpose is two-fold: comprehensive discipleship and comprehensive witness. Comprehensive discipleship is a call to love God fully, with heart, mind, body, soul, and strength. Comprehensive witness is a life dedicated to making every thought captive to the obedience of Christ. I consider this two-fold purpose to be of utmost importance for my own discipline, theology. But I submit that all Christian scholarship, regardless of the specific academic discipline, should contribute to comprehensive discipleship and comprehensive witness.

The two-fold purpose of Christian scholarship requires that it be a shared task. It cannot be done by one person, or even a single group of people. That is why it is important for us to understand who, today, may share in the task of Christian scholarship. This brings us to the second part of the presentation, namely the shape of contemporary world Christianity.

Contemporary World Christianity: Where is the Center?

Several years ago a hamburger commercial in the United States had the question: "Where's the beef?" The Americans among us (since you are commercially driven) may remember that commercial. At any rate, the question is: "Where is the beef of world Christianity?" The short answer is: "It is not where it used to be!" Today, the Christian community is wider. We know, thanks to the works of numerous scholars (mostly missiologists and historians of world Christianity), that the Christian faith is no longer the faith of white Western people alone. David Barrett, Dana Robert, Wilbert Shenk, Lamin Sanneh, Andrew Walls, and Kwame Bediako (to name only these) have taught us that the center of gravity of world Christianity has shifted to the South.

Missiologists have known this fact for a long time even though it may surprise the general population as well as many Christians. Indeed, in his 1989 *Friends of St. Colm's Public Lecture*, Professor Andrew F. Walls stated that "the twentieth century has seen the most staggering development in the church for at least a millennium."[3] For Professor Walls this "most staggering development" is the result of two major changes: the de-Christianization of the West and the Christianization of the non-Western world. Walls provides the following statistical evidence: "In 1900, 83% of the world's Christians lived in North America and Europe. Today [in 1989], something approaching 60% live in Africa, Asia, Latin America and the Pacific."[4] Note that this change occurred in less than a century. No wonder Walls could only come to the conclusion that "we have seen a massive change in the centre of gravity of the Christian faith, so that Africa has become one of its heartlands."[5] I sometimes refer to the change in world Christianity as the literal darkening of Christianity's complexion.

The published literature on the southward shift of Christianity's center of gravity tells only *part* of the story, for the darkening of Christianity's complexion cannot be fully documented in published form. For one thing, some of the documentation will remain inaccessible to scholars who read European languages exclusively. This is the case for documentation on grassroots Christianity in Africa written in African languages. Moreover, much of the story of global Christianity remains untold. Commenting on the African situation specifically, Kwame Bediako suggests that "African Christianity must be distinguished from the literature on African Christianity."[6] Similarly, world Christianity must be distinguished from the literature on world Christianity. Nevertheless, the literature on global Christianity informs us sufficiently that things have changed dramatically. The change implies an increasing non-Western imprint on the Christian religion as the church becomes "a multitude of local movements for whom Christianity represents a particular culture's grappling with the nature of divine reality."[7] We must, for this reason, keep in mind that "[w]hat at first glance appears to be the largest world religion is in fact the ultimate local religion."[8] It can therefore be argued that Christianity is a world religion because it is a local religion, one whose strength "lies in its creative interweaving of the warp of a world religion with the woof of its local contexts."[9]

The shift of Christianity's center of gravity is good news because it means that, as a global reality, the Christian faith is increasingly at home in many cultures and will not be imprisoned by any single one. The good news, in this case, is that since "people of color" now represent the majority of Christians in the world, the perception of Christianity as a Western religion can be corrected. Making the case for Christianity on the basis of its being a global religion can, especially in Africa, erase the stigma of Christianity being a white man's religion. This will bring about apologetic dividends not only for Christians in Africa, but also for those in Asia and Latin America and the Pacific Islands. By apologetic dividends I mean that if Christianity is "de-westernized," Christians in Africa, Asia, and Latin America are able to defend themselves when accused of being agents of westernization and puppets in the hands of foreigners whose intention is the destruction of local cultures and religions.

I am fully aware of the fact that many around the world continue to perceive Christianity as a Western religion. This perception does not, however, alter the reality that Christianity is now a local world religion. As Lamin Sanneh writes, "...Christianity as a truly world religion [is] increasingly defined by the values and idioms of non-Western cultures and languages."[10] Yet one would not know that Christianity is increasingly non-Western if one reads publications such as Samuel Huntington's *The Clash of Civilizations and the Remaking of World Order.*

It is remarkable that in this book, published in 1996, Huntington states, "'the West' is now universally used to refer to what used to be called Western Christendom."[11] This statement seems to accredit the idea that Christianity is Western, especially if one accepts, as Huntington apparently does, the proposition that "[r]eligion is a central defining characteristic of civilizations."[12] Western civilization continues, then, to be defined by the Christian religion.

I could not help but notice that Huntington does not mention a particular civilization pertaining to Africa. This is how Huntington deals with the African situation in his list of "Civilizations in History and Today": *"African (possibly).* Most major scholars of civilization except Braudel do not recognize a distinct African civilization."[13] Huntington cites many reasons for the non-existence of African civilization. Among the explanations given, one finds, of course, the usual idea about "tribal identities" being pervasive in Africa. But, what I find most intriguing and interesting is the following statement: "Most significantly, European imperialism brought Christianity to most of the continent south of the Sahara.... [C]onceivably sub-Saharan Africa could cohere into a distinct civilization, with South Africa possibly being its core state."[14]

What should one make of this assertion? Has the presence of Christianity in Africa obliterated African civilization? If so, how can a distinct African civilization "cohere" around one of the most Christianized countries of the continent? Moreover, why did the presence of Christianity in Asia not produce the same effects?

Chee Pang Choong, from Trinity College in Singapore, provides an Asian perspective on Huntington's claims. According to him, "'Western' or the 'West' is... used [by Huntington] rather broadly or loosely as a synonym for 'Christian' or 'Christianity' minus the 'Slavic-Orthodox' civilization."[15] For Chee Pang Choong this constitutes a serious problem because it only reinforces "the already common impression and prejudice in the non-Western world that Christianity is a Western entity rather than a cross-cultural and universal religion."[16] For Christians in Asia and Africa, then, Huntington's ideas only provide arguments to Asian and African critics of the Christian faith. This is so because

> [t]he Christian population in Asia seems to have been ignored completely....
>
> [And] Huntington seems to have failed to recognize the very important fact that the Christian population or 'map' world wide has changed significantly since the end of World War II.[17]

Major changes have occurred in global Christianity. These changes are known by missiologists and historians of world Christianity, but less known by Christians who are not in missiology and similar disciplines in the West. The "southward shift" of Christianity's center of gravity is hardly noticed or seriously taken into account by other scholars who happen not to be Christian.

Non-Christian scholars may be able to afford ignoring the shift in Christianity's center of gravity. For Christian scholars (even those in the West), however, ignoring this "southward shift" has detrimental effects. Christian scholars need to be aware of the change in Christianity's center of gravity because "the faith of the twenty-first century will require a devout, vigorous Christian scholarship rooted in the soil of Africa, Asia and Latin America," for

> the majority of Christians are now Africans, Asians, Latin Americans, and Pacific Islanders.... Christianity is now primarily a non-Western religion and on all present indications will steadily become more so....
>
> The most urgent reason for the study of the religious traditions of Africa and Asia, of the Amerindian and the Pacific peoples, is their significance for Christian theology; they are the substratum of the Christian faith and life of the greater number of the Christians of the world.[18]

In light of the foregoing, perhaps the question should be: Why has Christian scholarship paid so little attention to the "majority of Christians"? Is it because few Christian scholars agree with Professor Andrew Walls that "the future of the Christian faith, its shape in the twenty-first and twenty-second centuries, is being decided by events which are now taking place in Africa, in Asia, and Latin America, or which will do so in the near future?"[19] I wonder what would happen to Christian scholarship if all Christian scholars (from Northern as well as Southern continents) really believed that the future of Christianity no longer depends on developments in the North.

Acknowledging the fact that "the majority of Christians" are no longer Westerners is one thing. One may even concede that the demographic future of Christianity belongs to Africa, Asia, and Latin America. Does this also mean that the future of Christian scholarship is being decided in these continents? One cannot presume a positive answer to this question. Take Africa as an example. Kwame Bediako notes that "African Christianity has not attracted as much attention as its massive presence in Africa would appear to require."[20] Similar observations can be made about Asian and Latin American Christianities. Yet, Bediako is hopeful. In spite of the current Afro-pessimism and views on Africa's marginalization in today's world, Bediako believes that "in one particular respect, and perhaps in others too, Africa will not be marginalised, and that is in the field of scholarship, and specifically Christian and religious scholarship."[21]

I do not share Bediako's optimism fully. For me, optimism must be tempered by the following observation made by Professor Walls in 1991:

> In the last three decades literally hundreds of Africans and Asians have qualified at doctoral or equivalent level in Western theological institutions. Many of them did work of high quality in the process, and not a few contributed substantially to knowledge by their research. The expectation was that these would be the standard-bearers of the theological scholarship of the Southern continents. Clearly there are among them those who are standard-bearers in any company, who exercise an impact throughout the world. But equally clearly, the impact on scholarship of this corps of highly qualified people, taken as a whole, does not seem commensurate with their talents or training.... [T]he rule of the palefaces over the academic world is untroubled. The expected publications do not materialize; or they have little international effect. And this seems to hold even in studies specifically directed to regional questions.[22]

I realize that these words were written ten years ago. Has there been no improvement? Is the "Third World" still marginalized in Christian scholarship? While one cannot honestly say that the situation remains as Professor Walls described it in 1991, it is also clear that Christian scholarship is not yet an endeavor in which scholars from Africa, Asia, Latin America, and the Pacific Islands participate fully. Christian scholarship from these new centers of Christianity still needs to make its mark.

Christian Scholarship as a World Endeavor

The full participation of scholars from the new centers of the Christian faith presents a number of challenges. It may, therefore, be useful to review some of these challenges by asking ourselves this question: why, to use Professor Walls' words, is "the rule of the palefaces untroubled" in Christian scholarship? In my mind, "the rule of the palefaces" continues because of this paradox observed by Kenyan theologian John S. Mbiti: "[T]he Church has become kerygmatically universal, but is still theologically provincial . . ."[23] Perhaps this paradox helps explain why relatively few people realize that the change in Christianity's center of gravity "has not only statistical but theological implications as well."[24]

I contend that Christian scholarship will remain "provincial" as long as some major challenges continue unaddressed. I submit the following four challenges for your consideration: the West's "hegemony postulate"; the West's self-perception as "the center"; the perception of "Third World" scholars as "purveyor[s] of exotic raw intellectual material to people in the North";[25] and the "dialogue of the deaf"[26] between the West and the rest.

The West's "hegemony postulate" is the first important challenge we must face. The expression "hegemony postulate" comes from Per Frostin. He explains it in these words:

> In discussing Third World Theologies with Scandinavian colleagues, I have frequently encountered arguments of the following character: It is interesting that Third World Christians create new types of theology, but I can dialogue with them only on the condition that they state their critique of Western theology in a manner understood by me as scientific. In other words, the prerequisite of a dialogue is that the other party accepts "our" rules, since only these rules are genuinely scientific. This prerequisite for dialogue is . . . *the hegemony postulate.*

The West's "hegemony postulate" can be seen in other places. One may detect its presence in certain international gatherings. The "World Conference Against Racism, Racial Discrimination, Xenophobia and Related Intolerance" held in Durban, South Africa, is a recent illustration. According to Yvonne Scruggs-Leftwich, the discord at the conference "was fueled by Western nations' determination to have their own way and to play only by their rules."[28]

The "hegemony postulate" may also appear in statements about the West's contribution to the world. Consider, for example, this opinion expressed by Robert Royal, then vice president at the Ethics and Public Policy Center in Washington, DC:

> Despite its many shortcomings and occasional atrocities, this Western dominance is providential. No better champion of Justice, fairness, liberty, truth, and human flourishing exists than the complex and poorly known entity we call Western Civilization. The West, in the broadest sense of the term, produced both the New Testament and the Marquis de Sade, Francis of Assisi and Hitler. Yet its rise has, in the main, been a blessing to the human race. The West's weakening or demise would pose a threat to many human virtues. Recovering and extending Western principles remain our best hope for a more humane world. For in these matters, there is no serious rival to the West.[29]

How does this view of providential Western dominance affect the participation of the "Third World" in Christian scholarship? This view affects Christian scholarship whether its proponents are Christian or non-Christian. Can "Third World" Christian scholarship be taken seriously by Christians, especially those in the West, who hold such a view? We may find a clue in what happened in the 1998 Lambeth Conference. African and Asian bishops were the majority at the 1998 Lambeth Conference of the worldwide Anglican Communion. Yet, this did not prevent Bishop Spong of Newark, New Jersey, from dismissing the views of African bishops on human sexuality. As Lamin Sanneh reports, "he called those who did not agree with his progressive view on the subject backward and primitive in their reading of Scripture."[30] Bishop Spong's attitude illustrates the "hegemony postulate" as well as the West's self-perception as the center. This self-perception is the second challenge we will examine.

The West's self-perception as the center of scholarship is a corollary of the "hegemony postulate." Here the assumption is that the West represents the center of scholarship and the rest (usually Africa, Asia, and Latin America) fit in the margins. I see this assumption at work in the reflex of dismissing "Third World" scholarship without a real or adequate basis. So, for example, a seminary president in the United States can declare an African seminary "not a real seminary." I have encountered this on numerous occasions. The most recent one relates specifically to the West Africa Alliance Seminary, a seminary in Abidjan, Côte d'Ivoire. This is a seminary I helped establish in 1993. I was dismayed to hear that a U.S. seminary president made this remark about it: "This school they call 'seminary' in Abidjan is not a real seminary." My immediate question was: How does he know? He had not visited the school at the time. As far as I know, he does not know French and is not acquainted with the details of academic life in the Francophone world. I find this remark puzzling. What is a "real seminary"? How does one determine its "reality" from a distance?

The West's self-perception as the center of scholarship is not limited to theology and Christian scholarship. It affects many academic disciplines. Commenting on literary studies, Christopher L. Miller writes: "this figure of the marginalized Africanist: it is largely true to life. My contention is that Africa has been allowed to contribute almost nothing to the Western academy up to the present moment."[31]

Miller observes that "[b]efore the 1960s, Africa had been almost exclusively the province of anthropologists. Africans were seen more as cultural objects than as producers of cultural interpretations."[32] We must not think that this view of Africans has disappeared completely. African scholars encounter it in Western academic institutions as they discover the contributions they are expected to bring. The nature of this contribution constitutes the third challenge.

Many "Third World" Christian scholars have experienced the frustration of realizing that their contribution to the Western academy is that of "purveyor[s] of exotic raw intellectual material to people in the North."[33] The real value of an African scholar to a Christian college, seminary, or university may have more to do with his or her *Africanness* than with expertise in a particular discipline. So, African scholars are forever asked to provide African comments and illustrations on all sorts of things. The Africans' scholarly expertise suffers in the long run. Consequently,

> despite individual achievements and reputations, African scholarship is at best marginal, and at worst nonexistent, in the total economy of intellectual and scientific endeavor in the world today....
>
> [W]e have no choice but to produce what is ultimately a derived discourse.[34]

This is a case of inclusion by marginalization. As long as this attitude persists in Christian circles, Christian scholarship cannot be a world endeavor.

The "rule of the palefaces" continues in Christian scholarship for a fourth reason: the "dialogue of the deaf" between the West and the rest. In his *Cultural Forces in World Politics*, published in 1990, Ali Mazrui observed that America and the Third World are engaged in a "dialogue of the deaf." I think that this characterization is applicable to the relationship between Western Christian scholars and those in Africa, Asia, and Latin America. Mazrui contends that "Americans are brilliant communicators but bad listeners."[35] America's "bad listening" skills prevents her from hearing the Third World. I am wondering if Western Christian scholars are better listeners than Mazrui's America. If they were, they would not continue the practice of marginalizing Third World scholarship.

According to Mazrui, the "dialogue of the deaf" between America and the Third World is the result of what he calls "six languages of American policy" towards the Third World. The sixth language, the English language,[36] is the most relevant to our concerns here. English seems to be the language of global Christianity; it dominates international Christian conferences. Does English not dominate Christian scholarship? Can scholarship become truly global with one language in control?

The "dialogue of the deaf" between the West and the rest is still real. I see it in the remarks made by Italian Prime Minister Silvio Berlusconi in Berlin on September 26, 2001. The *Chicago Tribune* reports him to have said,

> 'We should be conscious of the superiority of our civilization, which consists of a value system that has given people widespread prosperity in those countries that embrace it, and guarantees respect for human rights and religion. This respect certainly does not exist in the Islamic countries.'
>
> The Italian Prime Minister added that he hoped 'the West will continue to conquer peoples, like it conquered communism.'[37]

Even though Berlusconi has tried to offer some clarifications, he nevertheless revealed "bad listening" to the Islamic world. This "bad listening" and the changed center of gravity of Christianity are the present real contexts of Christian scholarship.

Concluding Remarks

Authentic Christian scholarship and provincialism are incompatible. We can, therefore, ill afford to continue on a path where we have colliding "arrogant regionalisms"[38] in current world Christian scholarship. Let us, then, move forward in Christian scholarship as truly belonging together. But how do we do so? Habits formed over years, and even centuries, cannot change overnight. The change will require specific actions. One such action may be for Northern (Western) scholars and potential scholars to learn Southern languages (even minority ones) well enough to engage in scholarship not from a position of strength and power but from a position of humility. I wonder, for example, if the attitudes of American theologians would be the same if they learned their Hebrew and Greek through the Mali language of Bobo rather than through the world language of English.

Another way forward is for us to engage in sustained international and interdisciplinary scholarship on matters affecting all of us. Christian identity can be a matter worth our consideration. Now, more than ever, "the question of Christian identity is . . . a global one."[39] Reflection on Christian identity is urgent in light of the complex issues raised by the change in Christianity's center of gravity.

---

[1] James W. Sire, *Discipleship of the Mind: Learning to Love God in the Ways We Think* (Downers Grove, IL: InterVarsity Press, 1990), 15. Sire also states: "The Christian mind begins with an attitude" (24).

[2] See Dietrich Bonhoeffer, *Life Together*, trans. John W. Doberstein (New York: Harper & Brothers, Publishers, 1954).

[3] Andrew F. Walls, *The Significance of Christianity in Africa*, Friends of St. Colm Public Lecture, 1989 (Edinburgh: St. Colm's College, 1989), 2. It is worth noting that readers of non-academic publications have similar information available to them. For instance *Christianity Today* featured the globalization of the Christian Church in its November 16, 1998 issue with several articles dedicated to the theme "Now That We're Global." In the general press, *Time* (Europe) focused on the growth of Christianity in Africa (7 February 2000).

[4] Walls, *The Significance of Christianity in Africa*, 3.

[5] Walls, *The Significance of Christianity in Africa*, 3.

[6] Kwame Bediako, "Urgent Questions Concerning Christianity in Africa: Some Reflections on A Manifesto" (unpublished paper, n. d.), 1-2.

[7] Dana L. Robert, "Shifting Southward: Global Christianity Since 1945," *International Bulletin of Missionary Research* 24, no. 2 (2000): 56.

[8] Robert, 56.

[9] Robert, 56.

[10] Lamin Sanneh, "Christianity: Missionary Enterprise," in *Encyclopedia of Africa South of the Sahara* (New York: Charles Scribner's Sons, 1997), 1:296. Dana Robert ("Shifting Southward," 56, 57) and Andrew Walls (*The Significance of Christianity in Africa*, 3) make similar statements.

[11] Samuel P. Huntington, *The Clash of Civilizations and the Remaking of World Order* (New York: Simon and Schuster, 1996), 46.

[12] Huntington, 47.

13 Huntington, 47. Italics in the original.

14 Huntington, 47.

15 Chee Pang Choong, "Samuel Huntington's Clash of Civilizations and Its Implications for Christian Identity in Asia," in *A Global Faith: Essays on Evangelicalism and Globalization,* ed. Mark Hutchinson and Ogbu Kalu (Sydney: Centre for the Study of Australian Christianity, 1998), 222.

16 Chee Pang Choong, 222.

17 Chee Pang Choong, 223.

18 Andrew F. Walls, "Old Athens and New Jerusalem: Some Signposts for Christian Scholarship in the Early History of Mission Studies," *International Bulletin of Missionary Research* 21, no. 4 (1997): 153.

19 Walls, *The Significance of Christianity in Africa,* 3.

20 Kwame Bediako, *Christianity in Africa: The Renewal of a Non-Western Religion* (Maryknoll: Orbis Books, 1995), 263.

21 Bediako, *Christianity in Africa,* 253.

22 Andrew F. Walls, "Structural Problems in Mission Studies," *International Bulletin of Missionary Research* 15, no. 4 (1991): 152.

23 John S. Mbiti, "Theological Impotence and the Universality of the Church," in *Mission Trends No. 3: Third World Theologies,* ed. Gerald H. Anderson and Thomas F. Stransky (New York: Paulist Press; Grand Rapids, MI: Wm. B. Eerdmans Publishing Co, 1976), 8.

24 Per Frostin, "The Hermeneutics of the Poor–The Epistemological 'Break' in Third World Theologies," *Studia Theologica* 39, no. 2 (1985): 127. The article is an adaptation of a paper delivered at the 7th Nordic Systematic Theology Congress in Copenhagen in 1983.

25 Patrick A. Kalilombe, "How Do We Share 'Third World' Christian Insights in Europe?" *AFER: African Ecclesial Review* 40, no. 1 (1998): 19.

26 The expression comes from the title of chapter 6, "America and the Third World: A Dialogue of the Deaf" in Ali A. Mazrui's *Cultural Forces in World Politics* (London: James Currey; Nairobi: Heinemann Kenya; Portsmouth, NH: Heinemann, 1990), 116-128.

27 Frostin, 131. Italics in the original.

28 Yvonne Scruggs-Leftwich, "Racism, terror: A connection?" *Chicago Tribune,* 26 September 2001, Sec. 8.

29 Robert Royal, "Who Put the West in Western Civilization?" *The Intercollegiate Review* 33, no. 2 (1998): 17.

30 Lamin Sanneh, "The 1998 Lambeth: Conflict and Consensus," *Christians and Scholarship* 2, no. 3 (1998): 4.

31 Christopher L. Miller, "Literary Studies and African Literature: The Challenge of Intercultural Literacy," in *Africa and the Disciplines: The Contributions of Research in Africa to the Social Sciences and Humanities,* ed. Robert H. Bates, V. Y. Mudimbe, and Jean O'Barr (Chicago: The University of Chicago Press, 1993), 220.

32 Miller, 219.

33 See Kalilombe, 12-20.

34 Abiola Irele, "The African Scholar: Is black Africa entering the Dark Ages of scholarship?" *Transition* 51 (1991): 63, 64.

35 Mazrui, 116. The entire chapter, entitled "America and the Third World: A Dialogue of the Deaf" (116-128) is worth careful reading.

36 See Mazrui, 116, 118.

37 Uli Schmetzer, "Leader says Islam is inferior to West," *Chicago Tribune,* 28 September 2001, Sec. 1.

38 Philippe Quéau, "Un mythe fondateur pour la mondialisation," *Le Monde* (17 février 2001); 14.

39 Chee Pang Choong, 225.

Notes on Contributors

Joel Carpenter, Provost, Calvin College

Joel Carpenter has been the provost at Calvin College since 1996. He taught history at Trinity College and at Wheaton College, and was the director of the Religion Program of The Pew Charitable Trusts. He is a well-regarded historian of American Christianity whose best-known work is the award-winning *Revive Us Again: The Reawakening of American Fundamentalism.*

Elizabeth Conde-Frazier, Assistant Professor of Religious Education, Claremont School of Theology

Elizabeth Conde-Frazier was a bilingual teacher in New York City for several years before responding to the call to pastoral ministry in Brooklyn and New London, Connecticut. Before moving to Claremont in 1999, she was the director of Hispanic and Latin American Ministries at the Andover Newton Theological School in Newton, MA.

John Hare, Professor of Philosophy, Calvin College

John Hare is a noted scholar, lecturer and writer. He was the 1999-2000 Calvin University Lecturer and participated in the Notre Dame Senior Fellowship at the Center for Philosophy of Religion and Erasmus Institute 1998-99. His numerous writings include *The Moral Gap, God's Call,* and *God and Morality.*

Richard J. Mouw, President, Fuller Theological Seminary

A philosopher, scholar, and author, Richard Mouw joined the faculty of Fuller Theological Seminary as professor of Christian philosophy and ethics in 1985 after teaching at Calvin College for nearly two decades. He became provost at Fuller in 1989 and assumed the presidency in 1993. In demand as a lecturer, he has been a visiting professor at the Free University in Amsterdam and at Juniata College in Huntingdon, PA. He has served on numerous editorial boards, including that of *The Journal of Religious Ethics* and *Books and Culture.* Among his well-known books are *Uncommon Decency* and *Consulting the Faithful.*

John Polkinghorne, KBE, KRS, Former President, Queen's College, Cambridge University

Revd. Dr. John Polkinghorne is one of the greatest living writers and thinkers on science and religion: a world-class scientist turned ordained Episcopal priest. He is a Fellow of the Royal Society, former president of Queen's College, Cambridge University, England, Trinity College Fellow, and former professor of Mathematical Physics at Cambridge. His publications include many papers on theoretical elementary particle physics as well as books on science and theology. He is the winner of the 2002 Templeton Prize.

Marilynne Robinson, Professor of Creative Writing, University of Iowa

A scholar and writer, Marilynne Robinson is perhaps best known for her novel *Housekeeping.* The novel has been translated into nine languages, was the basis of a Columbia film by Bill Forsyth, and was included in *The New York Times Books of the Century.* Other works include *Mother Country* and *The Death of Adam: Essays on Modern Thought* as well as numerous articles and stories in publications such as *Harper's, Granta, Paris Review, Psycritique, Incarnation, Salmagundi,* and the *LA Times.*

Tite Tiénou, Academic Dean, Trinity Evangelical Divinity School

Prior to coming to Trinity in 1997, Tite Tiénou served as the founding president and dean of the Faculté de Théologie Évangélique de l'Alliance in Abidjan, Côte Ivoire, West Africa. While in Abidjan, Tiénou also founded and directed the African Theological Initiative on behalf of The Pew Charitable Trusts. He is a graduate of the Evangelical Theological Faculty in Vaux-sur-Seine, France, after which he earned the Ph.D. from Fuller Theological Seminary, and taught at the Alliance Theological Seminary in Nyack, New York. Tiénou also was the founding director and professor of the Maranatha Institute in Bobo-Ciolasso, Burkina Faso. His area of expertise includes missions, theology, and the church in Africa.